NONPROFIT FUNDRAISING MASTERY 2-IN-1 COLLECTION

HOW TO WRITE WINNING GRANT PROPOSALS + 7 FUNDRAISING STRATEGIES TO CONSISTENTLY SECURE FUNDING

JAMES RUELL

CONTENTS

STAGE 2
Crafting An Irresistible Grant Application

STAGE 3

Reviewing Your Proposal For Common Pitfalls

NONPROFIT FUNDRAISING STRATEGIES

7 Strategies to Consistently Secure Funding
And Ensure Your Organization Doesn't Fail –
Using Grants, Gifts, Digital, and More . . .

James Ruell

HOW TO GET A FREE COPY OF THE ULTIMATE 4-WEEK FUNDRAISE WORKBOOK

Would you like a copy of *The Ultimate 4-Week Fundraise Workbook?*

Get free access to the below ebook and all of my future books by joining my community.

Scan with your camera to join.

WINNING GRANTS

HOW TO WRITE WINNING GRANT
PROPOSALS THAT WILL GET YOU FUNDING
FOR YOUR NONPROFIT

JAMES RUELL

"Donors don't give to institutions. They invest in ideas and people in whom they believe."

— G.T. SMITH (PAST PRESIDENT, CHAPMAN UNIVERSITY)

INTRODUCTION

You might *think* they care—but they don't.

The truth is, it doesn't matter how worthy your vision is. The real reason most grant proposals never make it anywhere is that your mission simply doesn't align with the goals of the organization holding the purse strings. If you cannot effectively connect the dots for the potential funder reading your application, then you are essentially condemning it to disappear into a black hole of doom. The proposal you've pored and sweated over; poured your heart and soul into is all for nothing.

Your nonprofit changes lives. You know the difference it makes for those you serve. You know the potential impact you could make with even more resources to draw on. You know you need to raise more money and create more predictable funding streams, yet it feels like there is a mysterious code to crack here that you just haven't figured out. Maybe you've sent out application after application but aren't getting hits. You might even have a sneaky suspicion that something is lacking in your written proposals, but you don't really know what it is. You dread sitting down to write; it is a struggle to sell your mission and trying to do so feels so unnatural. Perhaps rejection after rejection has you thoroughly down in the dumps and reluctant to try again. The prospect just feels too daunting to tackle. You have hit a plateau.

But what if it didn't have to be that way?

Imagine having a steady pipeline of opportunities you feel confident about—a seamless process for identifying potential grants and effortlessly writing applications that hit the mark. Once you understand where to find grants and the processes that sit behind them, you will see exactly what you need to succeed. Imagine being able to sell yourself and your charity with conviction and clarity while standing out from the crowd. What if you could stop procrastinating on writing and instead produce winning proposals with ease? What difference would that make? Would you have the confidence to apply for the funding you never thought you could secure? How much more reach and impact could your organization have, and what new possibilities would open up to you? Imagine what it would be like to have more security for your staff and programs. When you have the tools and techniques you need, you will find a renewed sense of momentum and assurance in your own fundraising abilities.

It may not always appear to be the case, but the money is out there. The Foundation Center (2004) found that 35 percent of those surveyed funded 50 percent or more of the grant requests they received. Many even accepted and considered unsolicited proposals. You only need to look in the right places to start tapping into these opportunities.

This book will demystify the world of grants—a key element in most nonprofits' funding strategies. Most people take a scattergun approach to seeking grants, when in fact, what is called for is a structured process. You already have all the skills and talents to win. Now it is time to develop a strategy that you can rinse and repeat. I will show you exactly how to up your game and start consistently winning grants.

You will learn the basics of grants, how to find relevant funding opportunities, and the key stages of the application process. We will explore the why and how of putting yourself in a funder's shoes. This includes understanding their motivations, building relationships, researching their backgrounds, and then tailoring your proposal accordingly.

Then, we will get into the nitty-gritty of writing a winning grant. I will break down the elements of a grant proposal, explain each section in detail, and show how the parts all work together (complete with templates and samples to help you get started right now). We will explore how to position your pitch so you stand head and shoulders above the crowd, with ten practical tips to guide you in crafting a standout application. I will show you pitfalls to avoid based on the top reasons why funders commonly decline requests.

Your charity's goals may not be quantifiable by metrics such as sales or customers acquired, but it is still vital that you find a way to illustrate your impact to potential funders in a clear, measurable manner. They expect to see the impact of their grants and that the funds are being spent on the precise cause they were allocated to. It is up to you to integrate your insights and vision with facts, research, and numbers to convince them upfront and then to focus on performance measures and report back on outcomes in a timely fashion. Do not panic if you feel out of your depth here; this is the ground we will be covering in detail so that you are well prepared to back up your case.

Finally, winning a grant is not just about writing a convincing application. A key element of winning funding is credibility and trust. It is essential for any nonprofit to cultivate relationships based on trust, so we will cover ways to build credibility for your organization, raise its profile, and get wider coverage. Plus, we will look at thinking beyond conventional grant-giving and widening your horizon. No matter your experience level, and no matter the size of your nonprofit's budget, this book will equip you with the inside knowledge to write winning grant proposals over and over again.

I will guide you through, step by step, until you master what it takes to write a compelling story that makes it a no-brainer for funders to pledge their long-term support. You are going to learn how to make it easy for funders to say yes, so you can stop worrying about where every dollar will come from.

Leading a nonprofit comes with its own challenges, but the rewards are even bigger. For many years now, I have been the Vice-Treasurer and Board Director of an award-winning charity in East London. I have played a key role in applying for grants and improving our financial sustainability, and in that time, we have more than doubled in size as a result of winning several high-profile grants, taking on new service contracts with local government bodies, and expanding the management team.

My background in finance (honed at a trading desk within an investment bank) serves me well when it comes to responsibilities such as monitoring the charity's finances, creating finance and expense policies, and assisting with strategic decision-making. This deep involvement in the charity fundraising process has given me a front-row seat to what goes on behind the scenes. I know for sure that it is more than possible to build a sustainable source of income through grants with a systematic approach and a proven formula for writing proposals that clinch the deal.

Now I have taken everything I know and distilled it into the chapters ahead so that you too can start to raise more money and lay the groundwork for more predictable streams of income. The good news is, securing regular grants is a skill that can be learned. I will share insider tips on the art of writing proposals, common mistakes to avoid (this goes for both amateur and experienced grant writers), managing expectations in your proposals, and crafting compelling narratives that win your nonprofit the funding it deserves.

It all starts with getting the lay of the land: how grants actually work, where to find them, and the key types of proposals you need to get familiar with.

Ready to dive in? Let's get started.

STAGE 1

STEPPING INTO THE WORLD OF GRANTS

1

WHAT IS A GRANT, REALLY?

Let us start with the basics so that we are all on the same page. A grant is usually defined as a financial donation to a nonprofit organization for a specific purpose. That sum of money is intended to address a need or problem in a community. Most importantly, grants do not need to be paid back, making them an ideal source of funds for a nonprofit.

Institutions, either public or private, typically award grants, but the most common grant funding sources are government agencies (at local, regional, or national levels), corporations, and foundations. Individuals can also be grantmakers in their own right. Grants can range hugely in size and scale, from as little as a few hundred dollars to millions of dollars. Many are designed to fund specific work streams during a particular time frame, while others can be used to fund start up or operational costs.

Often, grants will be earmarked for specific purposes. For example, grantmakers generally focus on supporting a defined location (e.g., city or region), sector or population (e.g., migrants), or a specific type of nonprofit (e.g., educational). Grants may also be allotted to support a particular person, project, or program. In the private sector, grants are often targeted towards special interests based on the priorities of the donor, such as research into specific diseases or certain performing arts.

It is important to note that grants are not contracts. When you receive a grant, it is based on the understanding that you will use the money to have a go at accomplishing a specific objective that you have agreed to. While you would, of course, have reason to believe you will succeed, there is no guarantee. Failing to deliver would be disappointing, but there would be no legal consequences. On the other hand, a contract is a legally binding agreement. If contractual obligations are not met, there will be ramifications.

To apply for a grant, you would typically submit a written proposal to the entity behind it, outlining how you would use those funds and making the best case possible to support your application. That might sound like a time-consuming process, which it often is.

Although it takes time and effort, the competition is often fierce, and you will have responsibilities and reporting requirements to juggle, it is well worth it to go through the process and win grants.

If you have been itching to launch a brand-new initiative (like starting a new program to fill a gap) or expand an existing project to meet growing needs but cannot cover those costs in your current budget, then grants might be the lifeline you need. There may be a funder somewhere out there with cash to spare that is designated for the exact type of service your nonprofit delivers.

There is plenty of money being disbursed through grants by governments, foundations, businesses, and individuals. Over 900 grant programs are offered by 26 federal grantmaking agencies in the US alone. It is not always easy to secure grants, but there is no shortage of availability. You just need to find the right match.

To give your organization the best shot at securing funds, it is essential to dedicate sufficient resources toward grant writing and take the time to customize each application. While a single proposal can literally take weeks of work to refine, an experienced writer applying for a combination of new and existing grants should have a 50-60% success rate. In 2019, 75% of grant seekers who submitted at least one proposal won an award. It pays to keep trying and hedge your bets; 94% percent of those who submitted three to five applications received at least one grant, and that number climbed to 98% among those who submitted six to ten grant applications (Submittable, 2020).

WHAT GRANTS CAN DO FOR YOU

Winning grants can have a significant positive impact on your nonprofit. Landing extra funding can obviously help you achieve long-term goals that would not otherwise be possible to accomplish. Plus, in the process of honing your proposal, you have the opportunity to reconsider those goals and refine what it will take to get there, as most applications will call for you to specify your organization's long-term objectives.

Applying for grants represents a chance for outside funders to get involved with your mission. As you tell the story of your cause and impact to date, spreading that message far and wide, you are likely to gain more support. It is a numbers game. The more exposed people are to your vision—the more who know about it—the better your odds of drumming up support and resources from surprising places.

Developing grant writing skills is a valuable asset for anyone in the non-profit sector. You will develop a thick skin and a sense of perseverance as a result. The process can be grueling, with months of waiting before any payoff, and you may often need to apply multiple times before striking it lucky. That said, it comes down to much more than just luck. In the chapters ahead, you will learn how to boost your chances of success, so you can improve your hit rate from the get-go.

Ultimately, funders are looking to support nonprofits they believe have a good chance of success. To earn their confidence through a written proposal, you will need to sharpen up your budgeting, planning, and organization as much as possible and show a high level of competence. Improving your organizational management is one of those things that is hard to find time for day-to-day. Impending grant deadlines can act as an impetus to prioritize these types of process improvement tasks.

Receiving a grant from a well-known institution, like a respected government agency or foundation, can seriously boost your nonprofit's reputation. That credibility can then help you secure even more funding from other sources in the future.

How many revenue streams does your nonprofit currently have? Diversification is essential for your organization's financial health. Any fundraising professional knows the importance of maintaining multiple streams of income to minimize risk and maximize sustainability. Grants can help provide diversification; once you know how to write and win proposals, this can become a dependable avenue of money, so you are not reliant on a single source of income.

Grants can also play a significant role in funding growth. If your nonprofit needs help to scale up, then a grant can offer the cash injection required for a large-scale initiative that you might otherwise struggle to fund. Landing substantial funding can mean the difference between launching a critical program or continually struggling to do it justice on a shoestring budget. Broadly speaking, grant funds can be used in several ways.

- **Program-specific grants**

Program-specific grants provide funding for a particular purpose, as outlined in your original proposal. Often, these only cover running costs and will not contribute toward administrative expenses.

- **General grants**

General operating support grants, conversely, can be used towards almost any type of overhead. However, these are less common and often hotly contested because they have fewer restrictions.

- **Capital support grants**

Capital support funding is usually directed toward significant activities such as constructing a building or similar large-scale expansion. For example, if building a new animal shelter is on your organizational roadmap, then this is the exact type of funding you are looking for.

- **Research grants**

Research grants are self-explanatory; they are designated for research and often linked to a specific individual researcher.

- **Non-monetary grants**

Finally, there are also in-kind or non-monetary grants. These provide support in other ways, such as pro bono services or equipment.

You will need to be crystal clear on the type of grant your nonprofit seeks as you embark on your funding journey. Understanding the main types of grant funding will help guide your efforts to concentrate on opportunities best suited to your needs and that you have the best chance to secure.

TYPES OF GRANT PROPOSALS

What comes to mind when you think of this phrase? For lots of people, it conjures up visions of thick, multi-page documents. However, this is not always required. There are, in fact, several different types of proposals in the world of grant applications, and the most appropriate format will vary based on the specific funder and the type of funding at stake. Let's now look at the main categories to better understand your best option depending on your particular scenario.

1. Letter of Inquiry (LOI)

A letter of inquiry serves as an introduction and is helpful to see if there is a match when you are first approaching a foundation for funding. Typically, an LOI runs two or three pages and provides a concise summary of your project. In any LOI, you should aim to describe the relevant need or gap, outline your plan to meet it, and specify how it fits with the funder's priorities. You might send multiple LOIs to different foundations to gauge any interest upfront and test the waters. Foundations will generally outline their preferences in guidelines that are readily available on their website. Be sure to follow any specifications they have given.

Most foundations prefer to receive an initial LOI rather than a full-blown grant proposal. Why invest lots of time if it turns out that there is not an excellent mutual fit? It is faster for an institution to evaluate a pitch based on a short letter rather than an elaborate package. They can quickly decide whether it makes the first cut and then request a more detailed application if it does. If not, then you can both move on. It also requires less effort on your part. An LOI can be put together in a relatively short time. However, that is no excuse to throw something together without giving it much thought. This is your chance to create a solid first impression; just think of it like an audition or an appetizer (instead of a full meal).

2. Letter Proposal

A letter proposal is more detailed than an LOI and asks explicitly for funds. If you are seeking sponsorship or funding from a business, many corporations prefer to receive a letter rather than a long formal proposal. In most cases, three to four pages will suffice. Your letter should describe your project, give some background on your non-profit organization, and include the amount of your monetary request or details of your sponsorship proposal.

Although a letter proposal is less work to create than a full proposal, there is a bit of an art to briefly communicating your goals in the right level of detail: enough that the receiver can assess your request, but not so much that it overwhelms them. As a guideline, give enough detail to go on but do not offer more than is strictly necessary.

3. Full Proposal

A complete proposal is what you probably think of when talking about applying for a grant. It is the most elaborate type of proposal and can range in length from just a few pages to around 25 pages at the top end of the scale, depending on how much information is required. The typical format for a full proposal includes:

- a cover letter
- a summary of your project
- the amount of money you are requesting to support the work

Please do not skimp on the cover letter; this is a micro-pitch in its own right and needs to pack a punch. Funders often set their own standards or guidelines for proposals. Read any directions carefully and be sure to follow the instructions. Many grants are now submitted through online application portals, so take the time to understand how these work. It can be wise to write your submission offline; then, upload each section individually.

Now that you know the ins and outs of grants and how they can help support your mission, let's answer the next question: are grants for me? Grants are available from a surprising number of sources and for all types of causes, but just because they are there does not mean that they are right for your nonprofit. Before exploring that, though, consider the following activity. Please note, all the activities in this book are designed to spur you into action and give you the best shot of raising funds through grants. I highly recommend you take your time with the activities, put some thought into them, and complete them all to the best of your ability. Before you know it you will have secured grant funding.

CHAPTER ACTIVITY: CLARIFY YOUR NONPROFIT'S OBJECTIVES

We have already established that applying for grants represents a chance for outside funders to get involved with your mission. There is no way you will get someone else to invest in your mission if you are not invested enough to communicate it to them clearly. Writing a grant will demand that you tell the story of your cause and impact to date, hoping to spread that message far and wide so that you can gain support. To begin toward that, make sure you clarify the objectives of your business. Some people start a nonprofit out of a general sense of wanting to change the world. Others have been personally impacted by a societal illness—like a disease, lack of access to resources, natural disaster, and so forth—and want to be part of the solution. Others still want to give their financial and emotional resources toward a cause. What is your reason?

Determine your motivating factor. It will help you to define your mission clearly and to outline your purpose as well as the programs you want. While doing this exercise, try to create a mission statement as well. Nothing has to be perfect, or complete, as of yet, but you just need to start. Consult with any others in your nonprofit and figure out if your objective and mission statement is true to what you actually do. If you already have a document with your objectives and mission statement, now is the time to test them and see if they are accurate. Ask yourself these questions:

- Why am I/did I start this nonprofit?
- What wrong am I trying to right?
- What values drive our programs and activities?
- Where will we accomplish our mission?
- Who is the target beneficiary group?

2

ARE GRANTS FOR ME?

In Chapter 1, we established that grants are wonderful. People give you money to do exactly what you love—sometimes what you have always longed to do. What could possibly cause you to hesitate to take such a deal? How many times in life does it happen? We established that grants:

- can give you significant funds with just one proposal
- give you money that you do not have to refund
- provide resources to do meaningful work
- come with prestige and boost your credibility and exposure
- can make it easier to raise money in the future because success births success

- can allow you to implement projects that would otherwise stall
- have no limit—you can apply for as many grants as you want every year

With such an impressive list of advantages, how do you determine whether a specific grant is a way to go for your nonprofit? Do you simply write a proposal because you heard that money is available? Think about this example for a moment: your group offers after-school programs for kids, and you are hoping to get more money for the programs. A local foundation provides funding for community groups like yours, but it primarily focuses on the elderly. To improve your chances of getting the award, you could create a program that involves senior citizens in your after-school programs, but should you?

A general answer to that question is "no." You should not do anything that will mean twisting your priorities, and definitely not if you have no interest in senior citizens. Perhaps if the new program design involving the elderly met your organization's needs, it might be feasible. Maybe you realize that it is an excellent idea you never thought of before. The question to answer in this chapter, otherwise phrased, is "how do I find a balance between staying true to my mission and yet not neglect other opportunities that come my way?"

HOW DO I DECIDE WHETHER TO APPLY FOR A GRANT?

This is not an easy question to answer, mainly because in the face of it, it appears like there are all reasons to apply for grants and none to support the opposite. For most people, the benefits of extra funding outweigh the drawbacks of the requirements connected with the financing. As you are probably aware, grants are not easy to get. First, you must know the suitable sources. Second, you have to write a proposal that knocks your target's socks off. These things take energy, time, and intense labor, and sometimes these labors are not rewarded because, let's face it, grants are competitive. Nevertheless, many people apply for them, for the same reason that you do. They consider the efforts they must use worth the fruit.

Of course, there is the fact that grant writing is learnable, which is the whole point of this book. You can learn to apply for grants and to do it well. You can develop the two main skill sets you need—the actual writing and the supporting activities accompanying grant writing. However, does grant writing fit with your organizational goals? As it is, nonprofits are barraged with funding opportunities, all having many requirements. Every funding opportunity is communicated through a request for proposals, applications, and similar guidance. Each has requirements for the prep and submitting of your application with detailed information about why the funding has been offered.

It is your job to review a solicitation document thoroughly and to analyze its specifics well before time so that you can pick opportunities that fit the predetermined criteria. If you are sending out many proposals, you can track the requirements in a grant management system to organize all the data you have to interact with. The process of deciding which of the many opportunities is the best for you should be systematic and well thought out to maximize your time and send out applications that match the resources and goals of the funder. Consider the following:

- **Does the project align with the funder's strategic plan?**

Every institution offering funding will have a strategic plan. Aligning your proposal to that plan is ideal from both their perspective and yours. Proposals that strongly correlate with the funder's strategic plan communicate that you will support the work and commit to completing it. The implication is that you do not need to apply for a grant if your goals and theirs do not match. As a rule of thumb, related strategic objectives will always be tied to the project's outcomes. Funders want to invest in something that has a reasonable probability of success.

- **Do you have expertise and experience in the project area?**

Ask yourself: is this project that I am considering a new or weak area for our institution, or is it a strong area? Based on the funder's goals, this is something you must consider. For example, if it is a new area for you and the funder's goal is to begin a new program, you might be a good fit for each other. On the other hand, if the funder wants to offer mentorship to others based on the success of your project, it may be a red flag for proposal reviewers that an area is not your strong suit.

- **Who are the proposed leaders?**

Consider the capacity of the proposed project leaders. Are they people who are readily available in your institutions or institutions you partner with? Have they led similar projects in the past, and how did they do? Will they communicate capability to the person reviewing your proposal?

- **What is the financial potential of the grant?**

Will the grant, if awarded, give you a return on investment? Will the funding be enough to warrant the effort everyone puts into the project? Might it cost your institution more than the grant is worth?

• Who might you potentially partner with?

Collaborations and partnerships are an integral part of grant funding. Some funders like to work with nonprofits that are partnering for the expertise and sharing their results. In such cases, their solicitations will require support letters from partners. In addition, they will want to know how a partner contributes to the project's success—a component that will require planning and forethought. A grant funding opportunity with such requirements may not be for you if you cannot meet them.

• Can you support the need from research?

Sometimes, it takes research to convince a funder that the need you are trying to meet is legitimate. It could be that they come from circumstances worlds apart from yours. In such a case, think about supporting research that shows the need for your project. What is the problem, and what caused it? What activities support your efforts to solve it, and how will you evaluate them? If there is substantial data from third parties or reliable anecdotal information, you may stand a chance.

- **How competitive is the solicitation?**

Sometimes it is not worth it to go through the hassle of applying for a grant if there is a very low probability of success. Determine how many proposals are sent in response to the solicitation. How many projects were funded in similar cases in the past? Be sure to check the funder's website.

- **Do you have the capacity to respond effectively?**

Other times, you may be dissuaded from pursuing a grant because you do not have the time to prepare a competitive proposal. If you do not have the support of management staff to help with submission, formatting, and the likes, you may want to hit the brakes. While at it, think about all the resources you need. Are your people willing to commit to making them available?

- **Do you have a rapport with the funding institution?**

Think about your nonprofit's relationship with the funding agency. Have you had previous compliance incidents with the funder that could get in the way of success? Is the solicitation aimed at first-time applicants?

Applying for grant funding requires a lot of effort on your part. People working with and under you can significantly guide you to get financing that fits your overall goals. Putting these things to consideration can help you determine if a funding opportunity fits your resources and time.

WHEN TO APPLY FOR GRANTS

Before you can apply for a grant, you need to be clear about what reasons are driving you down that road. Take a step back and consider the large picture. Why exactly is a grant a good idea for your nonprofit? Ask yourself the following questions and think about your answers well:

- What truly are my long-term program goals with this move?
- Could I possibly do the same work well or nearly as well without the grant funding?
- If I get the funding, what exactly will I use the money for?
- Do I want to apply only because I know that the money is available?
- Is the grant the best way or the only way to do the things I want to do?
- Might there be other, possibly better, ways to get the money I need?

- Are my chances of success realistic, and am I clear about them?
- Am I ready to do the work to create a top-quality proposal for the grant?

If you have a team that you want to rally behind you, this is the point to have that conversation. Involve your stakeholders in that decision as far as is reasonable. Honest and careful answers to these questions will undoubtedly shape how you proceed and who you may involve in the grant writing process. That said, apply for a grant when:

- You want to begin a new project or expand an existing one, and you need money for that. Apply if you cannot cover these costs with your current budget.
- You know of an agency or institution offering grants that pay for the types of costs or needs you expect to meet.
- You meet all the eligibility criteria for the grants you are considering.
- You can commit the needed energy and time to the process of writing a grant.

CHAPTER ACTIVITY: SHOULD I APPLY FOR GRANTS?

Take some time to consider the things discussed in this chapter. Is a grant the best way forward for your nonprofit? Think about the types of support available. Might there be better financial options to pursue? While at it, consider the kind of support you would want. You may find that the type of funding you need will change, or you might decide to get help for your work through other means (see Chapter 7). Perhaps though, you will decide that you really want to write a grant proposal. If that is the case, you can more confidently move to the next step in your preparation.

Make sure you create a working group. From the people you have spoken to about your hopes, you have an idea of who would be most helpful in writing the proposal. Remember that often, you will need the input of others in planning the grant application. Even if they may not have expertise in grant writing, they may have attractive ideas for the content, helpful strategic thoughts, or specialized knowledge, which you may not have. Even if they lack these things, a working group can provide you with the support you need to do the job.

Ensure that the working group you create knows the way forward. Make them aware of the fact that you would appreciate their honest input throughout the whole process. Talk about what needs to go into the proposal and how to present it (more on this will be discussed later in the book). The group will help you for a short period unless you are submitting a very large application. After that, it need not help with the actual writing—just to share information, exchange ideas, gather data, and do the necessary legwork.

3

LOOKING FOR THE MONEY

Now that you know the ins and outs of grants and how they can help support your mission, and you have decided they are the best funding option for you, let's turn to the next step: where to look for them. Grants are available from a surprising number of sources, and once you know exactly where to look, you might even find that you are spoiled for choice.

What is the first step for any successful grant writer? Setting their sights, of course. Before you even begin, you should dedicate some time to thoroughly researching the types of grants available for your nonprofit. However, if you are new to the grants game, it can feel overwhelming trying to pinpoint precisely the proper grant opportunities among all the options out there. This chapter is dedicated to the search stage: different ways to find funding and where specifically to look for relevant grants. I will walk you through the process of how to go about looking for grants and how the system broadly works, so you know what to expect.

There are grants designed for organizations at every step of the maturity scale, sector, and geographic region. Every proposal should begin with an audit of the landscape, so you can pinpoint all potential opportunities worth considering. Once you have done your homework, you should generate a shortlist, then narrow it down and pursue the most likely candidates.

WHO GIVES GRANTS? AND WHY?

In the world of funding, it is helpful to understand who is actually giving out money and why. Society is becoming increasingly complex, and donors' changing perceptions of giving reflect this. So, let's begin with a brief overview of various reasons why donors choose to fund grants or otherwise support non-profit work. For starters, you can win funds in the form of a large grant from a single donor. Donors give for many reasons. They may give out of a desire to change the world or give for personal fulfillment. Most wealthy donors are driven to make a difference in society and genuinely help other people. Tax benefits or ego boosts are a plus, but they are rarely the primary motivator. In the US, donor-advised funds are a fast-growing vehicle for charitable giving; donors make contributions when it suits them, receive an immediate tax deduction, and then recommend grants to their favorite charities. In 2019, donors recommended grants adding up to more than $25 billion to charities, according to the National Philanthropic Trust.

According to Fidelity (2016), donors are almost as likely to give because of an intrinsic motivator, such as personal values, as they give for an external reason, such as making a difference or meeting a great need. Although awareness of global issues is generally increasing, most donors believe solving domestic problems is most crucial. The challenges donors perceive as the most important societal issues to address for the future include:

- developing treatment or cures for diseases
- hunger and access to nutritious food
- access to basic health services
- protecting the environment
- access to basic education
- access to clean water

Individual awarding donors often fund causes that are deeply personal to them. These might be particular religious beliefs, political leanings, or sporting interests, for example. Someone who has close emotional ties to that organization or cause is more likely to support it regularly. For example, suppose you had lost several family members to a particular form of cancer. In that case, you might be more inclined to support a charity that funds research into the disease or provides practical support to those affected by it. Donors who have personally benefited from a service in the past or have a regular link to it because the issue is embedded into their daily lives are often driven to give back. They appreciate what they gained as a result of their experience.

Governments also give out grants. Various government agencies or departments often allocate these for specific causes such as housing, human services (e.g., for children or migrant communities), or education. It is essential for any nonprofit chasing government grants to carefully check whether their mission matches up to any government program.

It is worth noting that simply getting a government grant application ready to submit can be pretty labor-intensive. It may feel like there are never-ending hoops to jump through and the process is overly complicated. On top of that, short lead times are not uncommon. Once details are released, you may find that the deadline for submission is just weeks away. Conversely, the payout can be protracted, so the influx of cash may be slow to arrive. Government grants also tend to involve a fair degree of monitoring regarding how the funds are spent and whether they deliver the promised results.

On the plus side, many government grants are for hefty amounts and can mean a massive boost to your bottom line. In addition, government agencies often provide extra value to grant recipients, like assistance, consulting, or workshops, on top of the funding. Furthermore, they may come to consider your nonprofit as a leader in the field, giving you more influence when it comes to matters of public policy. Finally, being recognized as a recipient may open doors for introductions to even more potential partners or resources through the government networks.

Grants awarded by organizations often are geared toward solving big problems in the world. For example, Rotary Foundation aims to support projects in categories such as the environment, education, mothers and children, clean water, fighting disease, local economic development, and peace. At the other end of the scale, they might be focused on supporting local grassroots, community nonprofits. Corporate donations often look to fund projects or programs that align with their company values. Businesses are also often willing to donate goods that would otherwise go to waste, like perishables. By simply checking what causes a business supports or sponsors, you can get a good idea of what they believe in and are most likely to fund.

Here is a sample of the types of initiatives major corporates look to fund based on their gifting priorities.

- **3M:** 3M's corporate giving focuses on three distinct categories: education, community, and the environment.
- **Coca-Cola:** The Coca-Cola Foundation focuses on empowering women economically, health and wellbeing, and water—encompassing conservation and ensuring access to clean water.
- **Fidelity:** The Fidelity Foundation offers support in the form of substantial grants to larger nonprofits focusing on arts and culture, community development, social services, and health.
- **Ford:** The Ford Motor Company Fund provides grants to groups that focus on communities, education, and safety.
- **GE Foundation:** The GE Foundation's corporate grants are targeted primarily at health and education initiatives.
- **Goldman Sachs:** Through Goldman Sachs Gives, nonprofits that focus on education, communities, creating jobs, and helping veterans can all stand to benefit.

- **Intel:** The Intel Foundation is designed to support initiatives that advance science, technology, engineering, and math (STEM) education.
- **Nordstrom:** Most of Nordstrom's corporate grants are geared towards programs and organizations that prioritize and empower children and young adults.

Donors want to see the impact of their grants. According to The Guardian (2015), 58% of mainstream and 61% of high-income donors pay close attention to impact when choosing where to direct charitable funds. That is why it is so crucial that your organization's mission matches up with the funding sources you target. Today, the average donor is starting to more closely resemble an investor. That is, they are eager to get involved and to monitor returns and progress. Increasingly, they are willing to go beyond one-offs and engage for the long term. As modern funders are thinking differently, so too must the recipients of their money. This calls for a new approach to storytelling and evaluation. Kay Sprinkel Grace, author of *Fundraising Mistakes that Bedevil All Boards (and Staff Too)* and *Over Goal! What You Must Know to Excel at Fundraising Today* is credited as saying, "In good times and bad, we know that people give because you meet needs, not because you have needs." It is absolutely vital to get a handle on ways to effectively communicate the impact of your nonprofit's work if you want to maintain a high donor retention rate.

Donors today have more options regarding how and where to give, and they want to understand how their charitable dollars will be used instead of simply writing out a check and calling it a day. Consider the growing popularity of nonprofit measurement websites such as Charity Navigator and GuideStar. A Fidelity (2017) charitable study concluded that 81% of donors have questions or concerns about impact, ranging from unease about evaluating an organization's credibility to frustrations with those that do not always explain how a donation will be used. Further, two-thirds of donors say better understanding their impact would influence them to give more. Clearly, many donors struggle to get straightforward answers related to the impact of their giving. Most people understandably want to know whether they made the right choice in supporting a particular nonprofit or project. No one wants to help a doomed cause. If a program is thriving, then its supporters naturally want that winning streak to continue and will keep betting on its fortunes.

Keep in mind that many donors do not have a clear idea of what information they need. They just want assurance that their funds are going to the right place and being used well. According to Bridgespan (2011), past and current performance data, outside reviews from experts or testimonials, and feedback from beneficiaries are all perceived as valuable. They found that among the 700-plus foundation grantmakers surveyed, their top unmet need was an insight into nonprofit effectiveness. This group tends to consume relatively high volumes of performance information and is quite advanced in terms of what they expect to see, how they find this data, and how they use it to inform future decision-making.

However, precisely assessing impact is a tricky thing. Medical research can take years to pay off. Wicked problems like human rights and poverty may have no real endpoint in sight. So how do you measure societal change? In these cases, focusing on monitoring progress and quantifying benefits to individuals and communities may be the best option. Investors look for results at the company level. How do the numbers stack up compared to the previous year? But in the non-profit field, donors must take a broader view. In considering impact, we often look at change at the community level—or even wider. Regional, national, and global organizations operate at an entirely different scale. The horizon is also longer. Businesses are incentivized on short-term performance, while nonprofits typically work to bring about sustainable, lasting changes.

Donors are entitled to clarity about the funds they bestow. They also need to be realistic about what can reasonably be tracked, how, and by whom. Nonprofits have a role to play in managing those expectations. Today, many nonprofits feel the pressure of donor expectations with different sets of reporting requirements for various stakeholders. Both donors and recipients should agree upfront on what kind of reporting can be provided and at whose cost.

SEARCHING FOR GRANTS AND WHERE TO FIND THEM

According to statistics compiled by the National Philanthropic Trust, giving is on the rise in the US, increasing steadily every year across individual, corporate, and foundation giving. In the UK, grant-giving by the top 300 foundations in 2017/2018 was £2.6 billion, accounting for about 90% of total independent foundation giving. There's still more good news on that front. In 2017, at least 18% of US public charities received a grant from a grantmaker. Candid (2020) analyzed all $10,000 or more grants awarded by 1,000 of the largest private and community foundations, representing about half of all foundation grantmaking dollars. The median grant amount was $35,000, and a quarter of the total funds were awarded for international purposes. The top areas that benefited included health, education, community and economic development, human services, and arts and culture. Funds were directed chiefly toward program development, general support, research and evaluation, policy reform and advocacy, and capacity building.

Where do you start? An excellent place to look for grants is on official websites, such as US-based grants.gov (join the mailing list for a regular roundup of current opportunities) or grantsonline.org.uk. Simply search for funding applicable to your nonprofit by category. Depending on where you are based, you might drill down to the regional government level. Next, explore local public agency websites to see what funds might be available. Choose departments that most closely align with your nonprofit's mission. For example, that might be the Department of Education, Department of Health, Family Services, Arts and Culture, Economic Development, or Transport. Then, spend some time strategically searching Google. You will want to have a list of keywords at hand that sum up the need you serve and the work you do. Consider sector, target audience or population, gender, race, ethnicity, physical location, etc. Brainstorm lots of synonyms to plug in, so you know you have covered as many bases as possible. Then, refine as you go depending on the results you get.

Here are some other sources to investigate, which may lead to even more resources as you hunt for relevant grants.

- Candid.org boasts a comprehensive directory of grants offered by private foundations, corporate foundations, and other charities that you can access with a subscription—along with many other free resources.
- At GrantStation.com you can sign up to receive opportunities by email or subscribe to access their members-only database which lists funders that accept LOIs freely.
- GrantWatch.com is a search engine designed to help universities, hospitals, government agencies, schools, community or faith-based organizations, and research institutions find suitable grant opportunities.
- Instrumentl.com is home to a database of grants that you can browse by focus area or location, with full access reserved for members.
- TGCI.com, the website of The Grantsmanship Center, offers links to state-by-state funding resources, as well as a paid database of grant opportunities.

Think broadly when casting your net out. Who is giving to similar organizations? Where are your competitors getting their funding from? You may find fresh inspiration there. Also, consider asking your board members if they know of any grantmakers who potential candidates for financial support might be and, if so, whether they might be open to facilitating some introductions.

THE GRANT APPLICATION PROCESS

It is important to remember that every grant-giving organization will have different requirements. Pay attention to the details and follow any guidelines precisely as provided to give your nonprofit the best shot at success. Beware of any schemes that promise to help you land a grant in exchange for a fee. Unfortunately, online scams are rife, especially concerning government funding. That is a red flag if you are ever asked to hand over money to claim a free grant—this might be masquerading as a processing fee. Only go through official channels or websites. The typical grant process follows a general lifecycle, from the first announcement of the funding opportunity at stake, to implementation and review. The exact steps may vary from grant to grant; however, the broad strokes of the process are pretty universal.

1. Calling out for applications/proposal solicitations

The first stage begins with the grantmaker calling out for applications, advertising the opportunity, and inviting submissions. Then, as an applicant, you would review the criteria and determine your eligibility. If you tick all the boxes and decide to pursue the grant, the next step would usually be to register and create an account online. Then, you would complete an application, gathering supporting materials as required, before finally submitting a finalized proposal. Do not be fooled; this step can take days or weeks. You may be asked for information ranging from basic details about your nonprofit to in-depth explanations of the proposed project or program of work, along with financial data or other supporting content.

2. Initial screening

Once your proposal is submitted and the deadline for all submissions passes, the awarding agency will retrieve these and get to work. There may be an initial screening stage to ensure your application meets basic minimum requirements to qualify. For example, is the application complete with all fields filled out? Does your nonprofit or project meet all eligibility criteria for the grant? If not, it may be rejected at this early stage and proceed no further.

3. Full assessment and review

If your project passes muster, it will progress to a more thorough assessment of its actual contents. Each application will be reviewed and evaluated on the merits of program, technical, and financial perspectives; a cost analysis may factor in the amount you are requesting and how it matches up against the total pool of funds. How an institution chooses to conduct this review is up to them. However, a standard method is the panel approach in which a minimum of three people independently scores each application. They then reconvene to discuss their ratings in more detail. There will be policies to ensure all applicants are treated fairly and objectively and to eliminate any conflicts of interest among the reviewers. During this process, you may or may not receive updates on the status of your application as it progresses through internal stakeholder review.

4. Awarding the grant

The next phase covers the awarding of the grant itself. This tends to be the shortest stage in the process, usually lasting no more than a month or so. However, it is often an action-packed whirlwind. Once the review process is complete, successful applicants will be informed and congratulated. Recipients may be granted the total amount they requested or a partial sum. Next, the awarding organization will work with each recipient to finalize details and organize the release of funds. By this point, a significant amount of time could have passed, and things may have changed since you submitted your original application. If this affects your plans or timeline, now is the time to raise any issues. Otherwise, once you have reviewed your proposal, it is time to start planning for implementation with the disbursed money.

5. Implementation and closing the loop

The last stage of the grant life cycle is about implementation and closing the loop. This is usually the most prolonged phase and can even stretch out across multiple years, depending on the specifics of a particular grant. This is the time to send a personalized thank-you note. Then, with the grant payment now safely in your bank account, you can finally kick off that long-awaited project. It would help if you also started planning for impact evaluation in anticipation of reporting back further down the line. If you did not receive any guidelines regarding reporting expectations, ask about requirements; if they have no formal requirements, plan to send an update or two at critical milestones—sharing results, successes, challenges, and lessons learned. Stories and testimonials can also be nice touches to include. Schedule these to-dos in the calendar so it does not fall off your radar and be sure to add the funder to your mailing list. The final touch is wrapping up the administrative, financial, and program reporting side of things once the grant is entirely spent.

From there, you may embark on the whole cycle again once the next round of grants opens.

CHAPTER ACTIVITY: FIGURE OUT THE RIGHT GRANT OPPORTUNITIES FOR YOU

1. Clarify your objectives and create an impact statement

In chapter 1, you defined your nonprofit's objectives. At this stage, clarify those objectives and state them as clearly and precisely as you can. Use them to understand the work you do, explain it, and create an impact statement. At this point, your impact statement does not have to be perfect, but it must be clear. The idea is for you to have a full view of the work you do and how it affects your colleagues, employees, stakeholders, community, and the world at large. This understanding will help you when you are trying to figure out which grant opportunities to pursue.

To convince a donor to part with their money, you need to know your project inside out and demonstrate a passion for it. You must thoroughly understand the need or gap and successfully convey your ability to meet it. Your project or program should have been discussed and dissected, consulted on, and mapped out, with as many relevant stakeholders as possible. If you have any doubts at all, this will show through. If you are not crystal clear on whether or how the initiative will meet the needs it is designed to meet, then any potential funder will likely also struggle to see it, and consequently be less inclined to agree to funding. Grantors want to know why your project will achieve its objectives better than another comparable project would. They are interested in how you have developed it, why it has evolved the way it has, and who has had input into its design. If end users have been involved in helping to shape it, use this to your advantage to illustrate how well your nonprofit is tuned in to community needs.

2. Curate a list of institutions/foundations to target

Begin by visiting government websites. If you are in the US, visit Grants.gov. If in the UK, go to Grantsonline.

org.uk. If you are in another country, find the equivalent government websites and interact with the opportunities posted there. Be sure to join their mailing list so that you can always keep updated on what is happening. From there, visit your local public agency websites and come up with a list of possible grants you could apply for. Then, perform a Google search (or use other search engines) using targeted keywords. Create your keywords by combining words that best describe the work you do and use those too in your search. The following table shows some examples of keywords and the organizations or projects they align with. Use it as a guide to create your own keywords.

Type of organization	Possible keywords
organization providing food and shelter for homeless people (women, children, and men)	child services, adults, youth services, economically disadvantaged, food distribution, homeless, housing/shelter, human services
organization delivering food to the elderly where they live	food distribution, food services, economically disadvantaged, disabled, elderly services, aging
organization educating children between 4 to 18 years old	youth development, children services, child development, education, youth services, education

Do not be afraid to cast your net wide as you create your list. Once you have a list of say 20 possible opportunities, make a list of the funder websites and the requirements you can find at first glance. Your question at this point will not just be "could they fund our work" but also "are they people I am willing to work with?" They will be reviewing your nonprofit at some point. This is the stage where you review their work. Specify, using your impact statement and objective/mission statement, eliminate the options that do not align with what you do to remain with at least ten possible options. To make your work easier later on, make a document with the opportunities you end up with specifying what they need from you. Do they need an LOI or letter proposal? What is their submission mode? Do they have an online portal, or do you mail your proposal to them? Be as thorough as you could possibly be.

4

GETTING INTO YOUR FUNDER'S SHOES

You are a bona fide expert in your field and know everything about your organization inside and out. You can talk about its mission for hours and spout off statistics and stories without even blinking. It is only natural, after all. That is what you do all day. This is what makes you great at what you do. It is what you are engrossed in constantly, and in the non-profit world, coming up for air is often a luxury. You know how to hustle and get things done.

But have you ever stopped to think about what it's like on the other side, from the perspective of a grant-giver? What goes through their minds? What are their hopes, priorities, worries, or concerns? If you can begin to think like a grantmaker, put yourself in their shoes, then you will have a better understanding of what they are looking for. That means you will be able to better tailor your proposals accordingly to hit all the right notes. In this chapter, you will learn to come at grant writing from the point of view of a funder. Armed with this new lens, you can then start to write more effective applications that win out against the competition.

WHAT MOTIVATES GRANT-GIVERS?

Understanding your funder is an important first step if you really want to give your nonprofit a leg up when pursuing grants. Gaining a broad appreciation of donor behavior and psychology is essential for anyone who wants to write grants well and to win them. When you know the types of causes a grantor prefers to support, you will be better placed to get their attention, artfully frame up your request in your application, and thank them appropriately. No matter the size of their charitable budget, small-scale donors and multi-millionaires alike start from the same place. Their philanthropy is about fulfilling a purpose, and that purpose can vary widely. When done right, giving at any end of the spectrum should be equally rewarding for the donor. Every single donor should feel valued, be confident that they know how their funds are being spent and know the difference they have helped to make.

Grabbing a donor's attention is the first step in gaining their support, which may then, with any luck, blossom into a long-term relationship. Donors might be initially attracted to a nonprofit through a particularly attention-grabbing campaign, for example, then get to know more about the organization's streams of work. To give money, they need to trust in your ability to deliver on your mission and have confidence that their donation will be used wisely. This is an essential step on their psychological journey from awareness to conversion. Their giving might not directly map to the specific work highlighted in the original campaign that first made them aware of your organization's existence. They also need to be satisfied with how they are treated as a supporter. Your first opportunity to thank them counts for a lot; do not waste it. Approach it from the perspective that you are embarking on a journey to achieve a big goal together, and they play an invaluable part in successfully turning that dream into reality.

Assistant professor Jen Shang, who specializes in the psychology of giving and bills herself as a philanthropic psychologist, has studied thousands of people to learn more about donor behavior. In an interview with the New York Times (2012), she explained that charities can use specific words in their fundraising material that boost people's inclination to act in response. For example, women on average gave 10 percent more when solicitations included words like kind, caring, compassionate, helpful, friendly, fair, hard-working, generous, and honest. In contrast, male donors were more moved by words such as strong, responsible, and loyal.

RESEARCHING YOUR FUNDER AND TAILORING YOUR GRANT APPLICATION

Demand for funding is always high and these days organizations are receiving more and more applications for grants. This makes it vitally important to do preliminary research. Focus your efforts on targeting the right funders so that you are not wasting time applying to the wrong sources. This will greatly improve your odds of success. Scour as much information as you can dig up on every prospect to help you determine just how close a match your organization will be. Remember, having aligned interests is the single most critical factor when it comes to finding grantors. Many grant applications are turned down for the fact that they simply do not tie in with the goals of the funder.

Are you seeking funding to launch a brand-new program? Are you looking for support to cover general operating costs? Are you hoping to raise capital? Determine the type of support you need. In these cases, your most likely bets will tend to be foundations or corporations with an interest in your sector or subject area. It is also worth exploring smaller foundations, which are often more inclined to fund a local initiative or nonprofit than a national institution would be. Look for other potential sources of grant funding in your specific geographic area. Some institutions focus on supporting their surrounding communities. Others may offer certain grants that are only awarded to applicants that operate in specific locations.

If you find some hot local prospects, do your best to track down a personal link. The stronger the connection, the better. Perhaps one of your board members or top donors has a contact at that foundation or business. Do not hesitate to ask for an introduction—this will give you a significant leg up if you can arrange a meeting to discuss your nonprofit's mission or needs and put feelers out to see if they might be interested in providing help.

Once you have a list of potential sources for grant funding, get to know more about each funder. Explore their websites and dig into annual reports, staff biographies, and any other material that is available to find. Pay attention to their latest guidelines, which may have been updated recently. If you have questions that you cannot find answers to, then do not hesitate to pick up the phone. The more information you can collate, the clearer a picture you can build of each grantor and their motivations. That means you will have a better idea of how to tailor your approach for each funder, using common language that is likely to resonate and ensuring your ask is for a reasonable amount considering the context you are both operating within.

Too many nonprofits fall into the trap of spotting a potential grant opportunity and then try to retrofit a project to suit the criteria. If you try to shoehorn an initiative into an ill-fitting grant proposal, it will be evident. You should always be working from something that currently exists. If you already have a project proposal at hand, you do not need to waste time searching for examples, statistics, or quotes. You simply need to extract the relevant parts and summarize them.

The fact is some problems are very complex. A grantor may be worried about your prospects for success and wonder if you are being realistic about what is achievable, particularly when taking into account the total funding pool available and the size of your request. When it comes to scope, do not set out to try and save everyone. You risk over-promising and under delivering. It is better to set sensible expectations and then outperform them. Be pragmatic. Rather than aiming to decrease unemployment rates in your city, get super specific. What elements of unemployment might you be able to impact? A small nonprofit probably will not be able to single-handedly claim success in reducing total unemployment for the population at large. But you may be able to get more local youth into training or employment, or help stay-at-home parents successfully re-enter the workforce. Be honest about the limitations of your organization and its size. Your ambitions for impact need to align with the reality of the scale you operate on. Funders need to believe you have a good grasp of the challenge, your capabilities, and your role in the wider system. They are looking for specifics, not generalizations; they want you to paint a picture of the before and after, so they can visualize the changes that will occur.

Your donor base is not a monolith. Not all of them are alike and no two are identical. Some are wealthy and others less well-off. Some give regularly, some sporadically. Some are busy building careers; others have made a name for themselves already. Some are retired, some are highly active in the charitable sector. Clearly, communicating with all your donors in the same way would be a losing strategy. To effectively convey appreciation and effectively engage them, you will need to personalize your direct communications.

Enter segmentation. Any good database or CRM will allow you to record details about individual contacts. If you can start to group donors into various categories based on what you already know about them, you can start to craft increasingly tailored messages. You can then deploy more personalized letters and applications that appeal specifically to that group's interests, needs, capacities, and motivations. While there are of course commonalities that will span the various versions, segmenting enables you to customize requests that are appropriate and meaningful for each recipient. For example, you can segment by criteria such as:

- relationship to your organization (e.g., volunteer, member, alumni, legacy donor)
- donation amount (e.g., donors above or below a certain threshold)
- recency of last donation (e.g., within the last quarter)
- type of giving (e.g., monthly, annual, bequest, for a particular fund or program)

If you know that someone is interested in specific kinds of projects or programs, show them how their donations have supported work in that particular area. Thank them for their help to date and outline plans for the year(s) ahead that could be achieved with their support. If you are applying for a grant from an institution that is a legacy donor, play up the history of your nonprofit and highlight the long-term impact on the community you serve. Report on how any previous funds were deployed and plans for the next grant.

ENGAGING WITH POTENTIAL FUNDERS

Winning a grant is not just about writing your application for funding. To really lay the groundwork for success, you should begin the process of engagement well beforehand, building relationships with the people who are the decision-makers and guardians of grant money. Some ideas are simply best outlined in person, and some funders struggle to get comfortable with a new idea otherwise. An existing relationship with the grantmaker will dramatically improve the odds of having your application accepted. This may be a new approach for you, if to date your efforts have mostly consisted of sending off cold applications to nameless, faceless grantors. If you have not done this type of thing before, then the information in this next section will be invaluable for you. Learn what to ask a potential donor and how to go about building relationships and establishing trust, so that when the time comes to make your ask, it's an easy and natural segue rather than a hard sell. Here are some best practices to follow:

1. Make preliminary timely contact

Not all grantmakers have the resources to have direct contact with nonprofit representatives. But among those that do, this is an opportunity to seize with both hands.

Making preliminary contact is part of positioning your organization for a successful funding request. If anyone within your nonprofit has a connection with the funder, they should initiate the first approach. Otherwise, your chief executive may be best placed to lead the engagement effort. Sound things out within your existing network. If anyone you know has experience with the grantor in question, see if they are willing to dispense any insights and share any personal knowledge so you can get a better gauge of what to expect. In reaching out to corporates, institutions, or private donors, always remain professional. Plan ahead. Timing is important. Be cautious of reaching out before your project concept is sufficiently formed. If you engage too early, this can make it hard to speak to in any detail. On the other hand, leaving it too late can mean a wasted opportunity.

2. Explain the purpose of your visit and prepare

Make it clear that there is a purpose for your visit. In other words, let them know that you are interested in talking about your cause and any potential for them to be involved. That way, they will be able to ascertain who is best placed to meet with you and begin to formulate a response. Once you have made initial contact and your request for a one-to-one conversation is accepted, prepare thoroughly for the meeting. Plan how to structure the meeting—how long you will engage in small talk at the beginning and how to naturally transition into the ask itself. Do your research on the person you are meeting with. Do they have a history of giving? What concerns, fears, or objections might they have? What do they care about? What other causes do they support? Keep in mind that as an outsider, they may take more time to understand the basics of your organization than you might have expected. Your mission and needs may not be immediately clear to them. That means the critical question of eligibility—which is the main thing you are there to feel out—might not be easy to judge. If it's still unclear, do not hesitate to ask directly.

3. Practice, practice, practice

Practice every element of your ask. This is not the time to falter. To quote John D. Rockefeller: "Never think you need to apologize for asking someone to give to a worthy objective, any more than as though you were giving him an opportunity to participate in high-grade investment. Whether or not he should give to that particular enterprise, and if so, how much, it is for him alone to decide." By the time you are face to face, you should already have rehearsed the conversation many times over, playing out different possible scenarios. You should have your talking points memorized, know how to address common objections with grace, and finally shift gears into your request—which should be very specific and leave no room for misinterpretation.

4. Ask for feedback

Most people simply want to feel heard, so do not hesitate to ask for their impressions and input. Being asked for advice makes anyone feel important, and a potential donor is an especially valuable contact. One last word: do not read too much into these kinds of meetings. Do not mistake politeness or encouragement to apply as anything more than a courtesy. You may also consider feeding back directly to the grantmaker on the value of the meeting, whether or not you proceed with a formal bid for funding.

GETTING A FUNDER INVOLVED IN YOUR PROJECT

Ideally, your funders would be just as invested in your work as you are. That is unlikely to be the case, but you can still do your part to get them excited, keep the engagement levels high, and increase the odds that they will want to continue being involved over the long run. It bears repeating here that donors want to see the impact of their grants and that the funds are being spent on the exact program or cause for which they were given. Here is how to stay on the right side of quality reporting and regular updates.

First off, the grant money you were awarded came from somewhere. The grantor might have received it from donations, the government, corporations, or other charities. Just as you are accountable to your funders, they too need to report back to theirs and show that funds have been wisely used. They want to ensure they are achieving their own objectives. For example, if they aim to support animal welfare, they are entitled to check that the grants they award are doing so. They can then point to these as good examples of successful projects, which they might then use in their own marketing or PR activity.

Project evaluation is a key part of the nonprofit lifecycle. Evaluations help show funders whether your nonprofit is a good candidate for investment and that you are a solid bet. They are also useful for internal purposes. An evaluation can help you consider critically what turned out well, what did not, and what you might try differently the next time around. Try to involve as many stakeholders as possible in pulling together the report, so you can get an in-depth picture of the successes as well as the problems you faced along the way. Pose questions to yourselves such as:

- What were the benefits for those involved?
- What were the best parts and why?
- What issues cropped up along the way?
- What did we do to solve these problems?
- Did we make any changes along the way?
- Did the funding get spent exactly as planned?
- What might be done differently in the future?

AFTER GETTING THE GRANT: REPORTING BACK

The point of this section is to prepare you for once you get the money you have been eyeing. It is to make sure that you are just as efficient in interacting with the funder as you were before they gave you their money. The first step in reporting back is to clarify if there is a deadline for submission and if there is anything specific you need to include. Look back over your financial records and put together a summary showing that the grant funds were used to run the activities you said you would, including receipts if necessary. Grantors are looking for evidence that you spent the money on what you said you would spend it on.

Review what you pledged to do; do not stress if the reality did not turn out exactly as planned, as most funders understand that things change. For example, you might not have secured all the funding you hoped for, or you might have shifted gears to accommodate feedback from participants. Include a short description of the activities conducted, along with figures on how many people took part or were positively impacted. If there was a particular target group you sought to prioritize, mention how many from that segment benefited. We rarely know in advance how things will turn out, so be upfront about any changes in the plan. Pivots can demonstrate agility and flexibility. Show how you made the most of things.

Explain how you collected feedback and information about how the project panned out. If you can include direct quotes or photos (make sure you get permission from people first) this can really bring a report to life. You can run a survey to elicit quotes or simply reach out directly to people and ask them what the project meant to them. Then, record their responses. If those quotes tie back into the program goals, even better. Finish off with a succinct wrap-up that ends on a positive note. State whether you achieved your original goals as per the proposal and how it matched up against the priorities of your funder. You can also mention the types of work you are considering doing next, which is crucial if you are hoping to apply for more funding from the same grant-maker in the future.

This brings us to the end of the first section in this book. By now, you should have the lay of the land when it comes to grants for nonprofits. You should be well equipped with a broad overview of the grants landscape: how they work, who awards them and why, how to find relevant opportunities, and what drives funders. Now it is time for the part you've probably been waiting for. Next, we will turn to the nuts and bolts of what makes a grant application stand out. What exactly goes into a proposal? I will walk you through the various parts of a typical grant and show you precisely how to write a winning grant application.

CHAPTER ACTIVITY: INVESTIGATE AND NARROW DOWN YOUR LEADING PROSPECTS

By this point, you have a list of many potential funding opportunities you could explore. What you need to do now is find out as much as you can about them, so that you can rule out some and prioritize the rest. By the end of this exercise, you want to have at least five opportunities whose requirements you meet well and that align with your project's goals and roadmaps. Work on your list, from the first one, downwards. Call the foundations where they have provided contact information. Where someone in your working group has connections, ask them to initiate contact and connect you. Ask for information where it has not been provided on the website. Interact with the application guidelines and the grants lists for the previous years. Who received money previously? What amounts? Do your homework thoroughly— it will save you a lot of trouble and time in the end.

As you do this, you will find that some opportunities no longer suit you while others will appear more suitable. Arrange them in descending order from the most desirable to the one that would be simply okay. For the rest of the exercises in this book, we will work on sending an application to the grant opportunity that you ranked first. You can later re-create the process for the other opportunities. Make sure you collaborate with your working group as you rule opportunities out and rank the rest.

STAGE 2

CRAFTING AN IRRESISTIBLE GRANT APPLICATION

5

WRITING A WINNING GRANT

Even the most seasoned grant writers still deal with writer's block from time to time. There is nothing quite as paralyzing as a blank page. You may know all the facts and statistics but putting them together into a compelling pitch is another story. The good news is, developing a winning grant proposal is not magic or rocket science. Once submitted, you cannot control everything that influences a grantmaker's decision. However, you give yourself the best chance of gaining approval upfront by clearly communicating your nonprofit mission, credibility, the need at stake, your plan to meet it, and your passion for the task at hand. Once you learn the basics of this particular type of writing, you will be able to use the same formula to replicate your success time and time again.

This chapter will provide everything you need to get started in the right direction, including an overview of all the individual parts that make up a grant proposal, an explanation of each element one by one, and templates and samples to get you started right away. I will dive deep into the nuances of writing each section so you can portray your nonprofit in the best possible light in your pitch for funding.

GETTING THE BASICS RIGHT

Before you put pen to paper or fingers to keyboard, keep in mind the golden rules of grant writing. First, you need to nail your letter of inquiry. You will recall that this is the standard introductory approach required when you first initiate contact. This reduces the workload for both parties. There is less for them to wade through, and you do not need to invest too much time and effort into a comprehensive proposal that may not get read. Writing an impactful LOI distills your pitch into a summary with an attached budget. This gives the foundation a chance to express interest and gives you a chance to get a sense of your odds of success plus any adjustments you might need to make to your approach.

When the time comes to write a complete application, success will hinge on your ability to write engaging proposals. That means presenting your solution clearly, laying out the issue, and explaining your plan to solve it. Focus on what you intend to do rather than belaboring the problem. An action-oriented perspective should also be complemented with a reasonable dose of positivity; this is not the place for a guilt trip. It is easy to get caught up in the doom and gloom of wicked problems. Rather than focusing on all the terrible effects of underfunding in this space, take the stance that your nonprofit is doing outstanding work and will continue to do so regardless. Gaining additional funding would simply enable you to do more, better, and faster. Frame it as an invitation to come along for the ride. Focus on making a clear connection between your proposed work and the specific criteria for each grant, ensuring you adhere to the guidelines. Finally, ensure you are writing in polished, professional, and succinct language. Avoid jargon, overly technical terms, and using too many metaphors.

THE 10 MAJOR PARTS OF A GRANT PROPOSAL

Let's talk about the parts of a structured grant application to get familiar with the various elements.

1. Cover letter

Your cover letter introduces your nonprofit and proposal to the person who will be making the crucial decisions. A cover letter should aim to describe your non-profit organization briefly and its mission. Broadly explain your plans and how the grant fits in connecting back to the funder's stated requirements and interests. Clearly state the positive impact your project will have and convey your passion for the proposed initiative. The biggest challenge is keeping the cover letter suitably brief.

Always remember that your cover letter serves as a condensed version of your proposal. It should run no more than two pages; a single page is fine, too. Keep your cover letter succinct and ensure you do not repeat what is already in your proposal. The aim here is to convey how well you understand the funder and their requirements as well as how your proposal supports their goals. If you've had previous discussions with the funder already, make sure to reference those conversations; if you have previously been the recipient of one of their grants, express appreciation for it.

A cover letter should include details on the nature of your organization, the need for your project or program, the target audience, an overview and benefits of the proposed activity, the amount you are requesting, and how this will help advance both your mission and theirs. Do not assume that this last point is obvious. It's up to you to explain why and to get them excited. Assume that the person reading your cover letter is entirely new to your mission and write as if this is the first time they are hearing about your nonprofit and the work it does. Build in one or two facts that strengthen the narrative you are telling. Keep all your paragraphs brief and focused. Every word needs to earn its place. Avoid falling back on jargon and abbreviations. It can help to ask an outsider, such as a friend or family member, to give it a once over.

Start with the contact person's name and title followed by the funder's name and address. In your greeting, address the individual using the right honorific. The first paragraph should start with an introduction to your nonprofit and the position you hold there. Then get to the point and state how much funding you are requesting and why your organization needs it. Briefly summarize what your organization does, backed up by a statistic or research-based point that speaks to the need being addressed. In your second paragraph, outline your organization's structure, history, and purpose. Then, describe why the project at hand is important and how it aligns with the funder's goals and priorities. Finally, finish your cover letter with a summarizing paragraph. Conclude with a final thought about the impact this funding partnership could have on the target audience for your project or program. It's important to sound thankful and optimistic in your closing, ending on a high note. For consistency, use the same date that you will be using on your full grant application.

Sample cover letter

Jane Smith
Program Officer
Blue Sky Community Foundation
123 Hill Rd
Central City

Dear Ms. Smith:
We are pleased to present this proposal for your review and look forward to partnering with your foundation to expand our after-school programs. ABC Youth currently provides tutoring services under the Study Buddy program, which aims to bring all participants up to grade level in reading, math, and science. Many students come from at-risk backgrounds and are testing up to two years behind their age group.

During the past three years, we have seen significant improvements among those enrolled, with most students improving their performance by one to two grade levels. Building on this success, we now seek to expand this service to address the needs of the growing Latino population in the area. Our proposal requests $25,000 in funding to support the rollout of the ABC Youth Latino Community Pilot Program. This would enable the procurement of new computers, training for *tutors and facilitators, and a new van for drop-off services.*

We appreciate Blue Sky Community Foundation taking an interest in helping our students.

Sincerely,
Sarah Green
Executive Director
ABC Youth

2. Executive summary

The executive summary is a brief overview of the proposal with more information about your nonprofit, your ability to complete the project, the need being met, methods to be used, and how those served will benefit. Based on this, a grant giver may or may not read the rest of the application, so it's crucial to make a compelling case here. It is the first thing the reader will see and needs to convince them that your proposal is vital to the community, that your nonprofit has the background and expertise to deliver it, and that your plan is relevant to their interests as a funder.

Also known as an abstract, the executive summary is designed to offer the reader a synopsis of the proposal. It needs to be concise yet highly informative. Aim for four to six paragraphs in length. One way to approach writing your executive summary is to consider it from this angle: *What is the essential question you are answering with this work?* Frame the need or problem as a succinct query, then shift into providing the answer through your proposed project or program. What do you intend to do? How will you do it? Why is this work so important? What has already been done? Provide a brief overview of the entire proposal, including the amount of grant funding you are requesting. It's often best to write this part last.

The reader needs to be able to take in this section at a glance. Typically, funders expect to see the name of the project, the main point person and their contact details, and a short description of the nonprofit. Outline your mission, specific competencies, the purpose of your programming, and long-term objectives with a nod to the mission of the funding agency. In relation to the specific project that your application is for, explain the exact problem being addressed, goals and objectives, a summary of the project, and expected results including how you will measure impact and define success. From a financial perspective, include the total estimated project cost, the amount of funds requested under the application, and any other funding sources.

Make the executive summary easy to read in terms of both language and formatting. Use headings for each section and bulleted lists as appropriate. Write clearly and concisely, so that the reader can quickly grasp your key points. Take a high-level view and describe the proposed project in broad strokes rather than getting too deep into the details. It might feel like you and the grant-maker are on opposing sides, with you vying for funding that they may or may not choose to dispense your way. Another way to think about it, however, is that you both share a common goal: being able to point to a completed project and claim a part in its success.

Sample executive summary

ABC Youth was established as a 501(c)(3) organization in 2012 by a group of former education professionals with a vision for a hub of activities and support services catering to young people across four suburbs. Our center serves more than 60 youths each day through our programs. Our mission is to help all youth maximize their potential through academics, sports, arts, and culture.

We are committed to adapting to meet the evolving needs of the changing demographics in our service area. Our Latino Community Pilot Project will provide access to academic and social services to youth in the growing Latino communities served by our hub.

Program objectives include increasing the number of Spanish-speaking youth who access our services for the first time within the grant period by 35%, engaging a minimum of 50 Latino families through our new parenting classes, and increasing the number of referrals of Latino youth from our partner agencies specifically serving this community by 40% within the grant period.

Our hub plays a vital role in the lives of local youth, as evidenced by our 97% approval rating last year. Our service area has a rapidly growing Latino population, which has nearly doubled in the past six years. Many of these families are at or below poverty levels and have English as a second language.
We believe that this pilot will introduce our hub and programs to an underserved population. As a result, we anticipate a rise in enrollments, increased diversity among those we serve, and improved academic outcomes for them.

The total cost of this pilot project for one year is $50,000, and we have already received commitments for half of this amount from other funders. Your invest-

ment of $25,000 would complete the funding we need to fully implement this pilot. We are very excited by the prospect of partnering with your foundation and appreciate your consideration of our request.

3. Organizational background

The organizational background section of a grant proposal is sometimes referred to as the applicant description. Regardless of what it's called, this is the part where you explain what your nonprofit is all about. This is the space to brag a little bit, but do not overcook it. This section should not run over three pages. Only include information that will help establish your organization's credibility and convince a funder that you are capable of executing your proposed project or program. Make a strong case for why you can be trusted as a responsible steward of grant funds. Your aim here is to convince them that your nonprofit is financially stable, well-managed, has a clear mission, understands community needs, has a strong board and great team, is popular and respected, and does fantastic, much-needed work.

Describe your nonprofit including when and how it originally came to be. Who founded it? Why did they start it, and who is served by it? Share your mission statement and outline how all activities cascade from it. You can include a brief needs statement along with an overview of your programs. After explaining your organizational philosophy through the story of where it came from and its evolution to date, it's time to write more about the processes that underpin your activities. Include a detailed breakdown of previous major initiatives and particularly notable achievements that relate to the proposed project. A bulleted list usually works well for this purpose. Testimonials and statistics may be included sparingly to underscore a track record of success. Call out any awards or external recognition your nonprofit has received.

Be sure to include the full legal name of your nonprofit, its charitable status, physical locations, and a summary of the overall budget including past and current funding sources. Explain its position in the community and mention any collaboration partners. Make note of why your services do not overlap, highlighting the aspects of your nonprofit that make it unique.

Organizational history represents an important part of the proposal, giving a funder additional confidence that your nonprofit is qualified to undertake this work. After reading this section, they should come away with no doubt that this is the right organization to do the job and the belief that your team has the ability, experience, and resources to succeed. You may touch on the backgrounds of key leaders and those who will be directly involved with implementation with a brief statement about your staff, volunteers, and board, but avoid going into too much detail about organizational structure unless specifically requested. Focus on concisely summarizing your organization's history, current programs, and audience served.

4. Problem statement/needs assessment

The purpose of this section is to paint a compelling picture of a gap you have identified. If you research and present your problem statement well, this will go a long way toward supporting your request for funding. Keep this section brief—ideally one page or less—and avoid using jargon. Establish the need for your project or program. Outline the consequences of not funding the project and these needs going unmet. The trick here is striking the perfect balance. You need to communicate the necessity of your proposed project or program, without being pessimistic. Aim to convey a sense of optimism that your initiative will provide a solution to the need. In other words, it must be an urgent yet solvable problem.

The basic elements of a well-written needs statement include a general description of the situation that clearly and concisely defines the need. Clarity is essential. Remember that a well-defined problem is one that can be solved whereas a vague problem cannot. Provide as much context and history as you can so the funder can fully understand the issue at hand. Document the need, which should be well supported with evidence—as statistical facts, research, and expert views. Any data cited needs to be as recent as possible and traced back to reputable, unbiased, and authoritative sources.

Do not stop at simply describing the symptoms. Demonstrate your thorough understanding of the problem. Why is it a problem? Who else sees it as such? What will happen if it is not resolved? Identify the barriers to addressing the need. What is standing in the way of a resolution? What is currently being done? Once you have clearly established the status quo, paint a picture of what's possible. Describe the gap between what exists now and what ought to be instead. If your project goes ahead, what change will occur as a result? How will people be impacted? Be realistic about what can be accomplished within the lifespan and constraints of the grant.

Focus on the needs of the target population to be served, rather than your organization or its needs. If mentioned, these should be articulated within the context of the community. The hero of your story should always be the clients or community you serve. Help the funder understand the challenges this audience faces and how your nonprofit serves as their guide. In too many of our stories, we tend to portray ourselves as the hero. As you begin to craft your grant proposals, position your nonprofit as the sidekick. Help the reader understand the hero of the story and the challenges they face and how you will serve as their guide. Cast the need or problem as the antagonist. For example, if your target audience is children and the main issue facing them is economic struggle, you would frame poverty as the enemy and your social support programs as the solution. This will help galvanize a reader into taking action. Statistics are ultimately impersonal, but you can put a face to the problem by building in a case study. A real-life example of the problem and how it has impacted someone's life cannot be underestimated. Highlight an individual your nonprofit has served and who benefited from a positive result. Make it real by adding the element of human interest. Their transformation arc will be key to your proposal.

Sample problem/needs statement

> *Many youths enter adulthood facing a lifetime of poverty as a result of the environment they were raised in. Those who fail to finish high school are among those most at risk. "Their risk is greatest; their hardship is most profound; and their current and future costs to our communities are the most significant." (Moving youth*

from risk to opportunity - Kids Count, 2004, The Annie E. Casey Foundation)

Children from the poorest families generally miss out on exposure to books and other printed content, as well as the modeling of verbal skills—often relying on access to materials via public institutions, which provide unequal resources across communities. They have fewer books in their homes, fewer books available in their school and classroom libraries, and live further from public libraries compared to children from middle and upper-income families. This is compounded by the fact that some schools and teachers are simply not equipped to teach these students. (Poverty and Literacy Development: Challenges for Global Educators, 2011, Bernard J King.)

Illiteracy remains one of the modern world's greatest shortcomings. Not only does it limit the full development of an individual's capacity and their participation in society, it hinders them in everyday activities like reading labels and signs to less frequent but high-stakes activities like deciphering contracts. According to the OECD, adults with higher levels of reading literacy are more likely to be employed and to earn higher incomes. This disparity will only widen as information and communication tech-

nology continues to develop and play a larger part in society. (England & Northern Ireland (UK) – Country Note –Survey of Adult Skills first results, 2013, OECD)

Our programs are designed to help at-risk students catch up to their peers, improve their literacy and numeracy skills, and encourage them to graduate from high school. As their academic performance improves, so too does their self-confidence—providing a foundation for future excellence and success. We aim to ultimately assist young people in transitioning into adulthood, completing their education, and progressing into further training or full-time employment. In improving their lot in life today, we are equipping them for a more promising future.

5. Project description/Program description

This section is about making a case for support. Now that you have established the problem, what do you intend to do about it? Introduce your project or program here. Explain how this solution advances your mission and how it ties back to the funder's mandate. Make it easy for them to see exactly how you plan to tackle the issue by demonstrating how you have developed a thoughtful strategy to effectively address that need.

Include details of any steps you have already taken to remedy it.

Think of this part as your chance to make a broad case for your project or program and convince the grant giver to commit to financial support. A compelling project explanation includes a description of a community need and presents a plan to remedy it. When writing this section, ensure you answer the *who, what, when, where, why*, and *how* questions that relate to the project. Provide a summary of the work plan—what exactly is to be done—as well as plans to market and promote the project and plans to adequately resource it. A timeline of program activities can be incorporated into the project description. Consult the grant guidelines for preference, and if there is no separate component for plan timings, then weave it into this section.

6. Program goals and objectives

This section identifies expected outcomes and benefits in clear, measurable terms. It is intended to communicate that you fully understand the situation and have a realistic grasp of your impact. Describe the outcomes of your proposed work once funded and implemented, detailing the change you anticipate it will deliver for the community. This is where you have to convey that your vision is worthwhile and that your objectives are achievable.

Goals and objectives should tie back to your need statement. Aim to keep this section to one or two pages.

A goal is a general statement encompassing the outcomes your program or project hopes to bring about. Goals are visionary, broad, abstract, and difficult to measure in any objective way. Common keywords you may want to use in your project or program goals include *deliver, develop, establish, produce, provide, improve,* and *increase.* Objectives represent a step towards achieving that goal and are precise, concrete, and measurable. Goals articulate a bird's eye picture of your vision, and objectives detail what that looks like at ground level. For example, a goal might be to improve literacy rates in your city. The objective might be to provide 1,000 children in the area with weekly support from a reading buddy or tutor in the next calendar year.

One strategy for structuring this particular section is to break it down into direct subsections of individual goals. Describe an overarching goal, then refine it into one or more narrower objectives with specifics. Think of each objective as being a tangible result of an action, rather than an action in its own right. Structuring it in this way will clearly signal to your funder that your nonprofit fully understands its goals and can link those to realistic, actionable plans. Remember to check that you are regularly referencing your statement of need in this section to ensure consistency and relevance between the two.

Provide quantifiable measures for each objective and specify the target audience. Objectives could be focused on process and describe a specific output or focused on impact by describing an outcome. Ideally, structure these using the SMART framework: specific, measurable, attainable, realistic, and time bound. This shows you have put serious thought into creating your objectives and have a firm grasp on what is achievable.

7. Methods and strategy

The methods and strategy section is your plan of attack, where you take the big idea outlined in the proposal and carry this through to the reality of how you will make it happen. Whereas the previous sections of your grant proposal have addressed the *who*, *what*, and *why* of your plan, this is where you will more fully explain the *how* of your proposed programming. It essentially serves as the heart of your application and therefore should be the longest section—usually spanning several pages. This calls for a full explanation with details about the exact steps you will take at each stage and how you will implement them. Funders are looking for a logical, robust plan that will lead to the outcomes you have described.

You might choose to format this section as a chronological description with tactics tied to a timeline or, alternatively, as sub-sections for each of your objectives. Outline whom the program will serve, how they will be selected, and why this method is a good fit for them. Has this approach worked before for your organization or for similar nonprofits in this space? Are you using best practice or modifying it to suit the specific needs of your audience? Is it efficient and cost-effective? Does it work well for the nature of the problem? Describe the ways in which you will achieve the objectives. Provide a fully fleshed out model with explanations and visuals wherever possible. How will you execute the project? What are the key activities? Be mindful of any potential problems and outline alternative strategies you might deploy in response. Explain which staff/volunteers will be involved at each step, when they come in, and the roles they will play. Be sure to describe any partnerships that you will draw on, too. How are you preparing for the project? Are there enough people who are trained and ready to deliver? Is there board and community support? What other resources are required? Connect this to the time frame. How will you meet key milestones? Activities should be structured in a way that the project moves steadily toward the desired results.

Write this section imagining that the reader knows nothing about your nonprofit or project. Try to follow up any complex technical sentences with one that provides a shorter explanation. Continually relate actions back to the project's original goals and need statements throughout the section. In addition, mention how you plan to keep stakeholders and donors up to date along the way.

Sample methods and strategy

> *In order to achieve the objectives for our Latino Community Pilot Program, ABC Youth will employ the methods outlined below. Our confidence in these methods is backed by their previous use by fellow non-profit organizations in neighboring cities, where they have been tested and proven by Rising Stars and Active Alliance. We have consulted with representatives from both of those organizations, and their advice helped shape our plans for this pilot.*

> *For a detailed timeline, please see the appendices to this proposal.*

Sample objective

> *Increase the number of Latino-identifying students enrolled in our after-school program by 35% by the end of the calendar year.*

Sample method

We have already set up a working group to support this pilot and will establish an outreach committee led by two of our Latino board members who are fluent in Spanish.

We will hire two additional tutors, recruit a volunteer driver/facilitator, and obtain a van to provide optional drop-off services for students who require transportation home.

We will develop a formal referral system with other community organizations and agencies.

Staff will track students' progress at the beginning and end of each term. A program assistant will formally track each person's learning progress.

8. Evaluation plan

Just as projects vary, so too will evaluation techniques. Your approach will be informed by the measures of success you have outlined in your objectives. Failing to spell out how you intend to measure results can mean the difference between a successful application and a rejection. A solid evaluation plan has the added benefit of providing a guiding document and schedule for your team to follow throughout the project. If you are struggling to hit those metrics, this will help you identify the problem areas and adjust accordingly.

When planning an evaluation, start by considering what questions need to be answered. How will your team measure progress? What will define success? Set out some concrete, quantifiable metrics. Be clear about the short-term and long-term benefits, what information will be recorded and tracked, and which research or assessment methods will be used. Keep in mind the difference between outputs such as "implementing a new system to be used by 10 staff" and outcomes, such as "eliminating double-handling, reducing time spent on data entry by three hours each week." One is delivery-focused, while one is focused on results and change. Outputs could refer to the number of people served or number of classes delivered, and these are important to know for the purposes of resource allocation. When it comes to outcomes, benefits can include changes in behaviors, skill levels, attitudes, values, or conditions. Funders share your nonprofit's interest in outcomes and impact. Outcome measures can demonstrate real value in return for their financial support. They can also help your organization to improve your programs, develop long-term plans and budgets, and provide strategic direction.

Decide whether you will use quantitative, qualitative, or a combination of methods. Quantitative data is about hard counts; qualitative information explores experiences and feelings. Each has a role to play in different types of evaluations, and you may need both types, depending on your project. Articulate the reason behind your choice and ensure the evaluation approach aligns with your objectives and methods. Describe who will collect and analyze information, at what points they will do so, and how. You may conduct an internal assessment with your staff or hire outside expertise to carry out the evaluation. Qualitative methods can include focus groups, questionnaires, or surveys. Quantitative data may be gleaned from sources like scores on pre and post-tests or records of program participants. Along with end goals, plan for periodic evaluation at key milestones during the project lifecycle. At the end of your project, an evaluation report should be able to conclude whether the project or program achieved its initial goals and objectives. It should also speak to any changes made along the way and why, along with any unexpected problems or benefits that arose.

Your entire grant application should bring the funder along on a journey from introducing a problem to be solved, through your proposed solution, to a positive outcome. Make sure you have outlined logical steps to take your project from beginning to end, showing them how their input makes all the difference and how you will track the impact.

Sample evaluation plan

> *We have a plan in place to measure the success of our after-school program. This is designed to evaluate what information the students have learned over the course of the semester. At the beginning of the term, program facilitators issue a preliminary test to gauge a baseline and follow up at the end of the term with a similar test. In addition, at the end of each session, participating teachers are encouraged to fill out a detailed question-naire so we can continue to improve on an already outstanding program.*
>
> *The program is also regularly assessed by external eval-uators. This outside panel of professionals is working with program staff to create a more sophisticated process that is still practical to deliver and does not unduly burden the facilitators. The aim is to build a clearer picture of the program's long-term impact on participating youth.*

9. Sustainability

Sustainability is about finding ways to meet your present needs and future needs, using resources wisely with a view to the long term. Before investing in your project or program, a potential funder—be it a foundation, corporation, or government agency—will want to know how you plan to support your project on an ongoing basis. They want to ensure this particular workstream has a future beyond the window of time their funding provides. No funder wants to think that their grant will only cover a project for a short time. They are looking for long-term impact, not a quick win. They also want to know that your nonprofit is financially healthy and has a sustainable long-term outlook. Convince the funder that there is a way to continue the work after the grant expires. Will it continue to need the same level of funding, or will costs diminish over time? Capital construction projects have obvious sustainability issues upfront. A funder will seek reassurance that you can operate and maintain the facility once it has been completed.

Think of the sustainability section of your grant as the sequel to the story you have been telling so far throughout your proposal. How will that story continue? Where will you take it from there? Provide a roadmap that shows a clear plan for fundraising to continue operating and serving your community. Funders will be interested in both the short-term and long-term benefits outlined in your application.

Exactly how a project might be continued depends on its specific nature and design. Programs can be scaled by leveraging volunteers alongside staff as well as through partnerships and collaborations. Charging for services may be an option; this could be a flat fee or charged on a sliding scale based on individual income. Annual fundraisers are a common way to engage donors, as are membership and major-gifts programs. Naturally, ensure you are optimizing online channels and cause marketing to their full potential for giving. Corporate sponsorships —partnering with businesses on galas or charity runs— or employer-based fundraising campaigns are another avenue to explore. You could also consider potential entrepreneurial approaches that might generate additional revenue through selling products such as greeting cards or consumables and ventures like coffee stands, markets, or second-hand stores. Finally, account for other expected grant income going forward and ensure you are applying for all government funding—local, regional, and national—that your nonprofit qualifies for.

Any of these methods, along with any others you may think of, can act as effective strategies to continue to cover your nonprofit's activities. In your grant application, describe in detail which exact strategies you envision using. Include any information about hiring additional staff or contractors if that is indeed part of your ongoing execution plan.

At this point, if a funder has read this far into your proposal, they may have developed a genuine interest in your clients and the service you propose to offer. Now that they are invested in your story and vision, do not leave them hanging. Give them the confidence they need to trust that this project or program will go on and that your charity can remain healthy for years to come in order to deliver it.

Sample sustainability section

Over the past 12 months, ABC Youth has approached several new foundations for support. We are now delighted to report that we have received grants from the Northern Foundation (for technical assistance and capacity building), the Children's Foundation (for program delivery), and the Regional Community Foundation (for operating expenses).

Thanks to support from the Northern Foundation, we were able to hire an experienced fundraising consultant who is now working with our board of directors. Her mandate is to develop and implement a strategic fundraising plan, including an expanded annual giving program. Growing a larger base of individual donors will help to secure our financial future and diversify our income sources. This will complement our grant-funded streams; we currently have three

*active pending proposals, requesting a total of
$75,000.*

10. Budget

The budget identifies the costs to be met as part of your proposed project or program and the methods used to work out those costs. This will go a long way toward assuring a funder that your proposed activities are realistic and sustainable. In addition, a well-organized and formatted budget will make it much easier for them to digest and judge the financial viability of your application in order to make a decision. Ensure you have a good grasp of all the requirements of a specific grant before creating a detailed budget. Some will ask for more information, such as detailed overhead expenses, than others. Many grant givers also provide budget templates that must be submitted with the proposal. If this is the case, adapt your budget to fit within the provided form. Otherwise, the key thing to bear in mind when tackling this crucial section of a grant proposal is to be both thorough and realistic.

The funder needs to know exactly how much money you are requesting and where specifically you plan to direct it. This is especially important when you are approaching multiple funders. They may well be concerned about potentially funding something that is already being supported by someone else. Include any other expected sources of income; for example, you should disclose funds contributed by other parties. It can be helpful to include a brief overview of your regular funding sources as well. Your budget should reflect an appropriate level of anticipated funding from this particular grant giver. Do not give them a reason to second-guess your request. If what you are asking for is wildly out of line with the amounts they typically grant, you will appear out of touch. Likewise, if it doesn't line up with the scale of your project, it is bound to raise questions about how well you understand the reality of the situation. You will have a fiduciary duty to the grantor, so you need to ensure what you are asking for is within the realm of what you can achieve. Not only will this improve your chances of winning a grant, but it also means you are not setting up unrealistic expectations. Remember that you will have to deliver on whatever you promise once those funds are received.

Ideally, you would have a good idea of the funding organization's position and guidelines along with your initial project estimates, making this a fairly straightforward exercise. Document everything in detail; you need to clearly justify the level of funding needed to support your project. A seasoned program officer can easily spot padding in a budget, as well as when an application has underestimated costs. When finalizing your budget, go through your methods and strategies again taking note of every area that will require expenditure of resources. Include descriptions and hard numbers for each one. These could include staff and travel costs, fringe benefits, equipment, or indirect overheads.

OTHER SUPPORTING ELEMENTS

This section is for content that you would like to get in front of a funder but may not fit the main proposal. These attachments help them to get a clearer picture of your nonprofit or your proposed work. They can also serve as proof to back up statements you have made. Examples could include letters of support, resumes of key personnel, proof of charity status, clippings of media coverage, testimonials, etc. Do not go overboard; think quality rather than quantity.

Letters of support can provide further backing for the case you are making in your grant application. These are testimonials that speak to your nonprofit's track record of success and ability to deliver, illustrating that other individuals, businesses, and organizations believe you can get the job done. They show that others outside your nonprofit believe in the merit of your proposal. Each letter of support adds to the already compelling picture you are painting in your grant application providing further persuasive reasons why a funder should get on board. Although a letter of support will not necessarily seal the deal, it can certainly make your grant proposal more competitive.

A letter of support could come from a key stakeholder, a significant donor, a partner organization, a political representative, a community leader, or someone who would benefit from the service you would be providing. The stronger the reputation of the individual or organization providing the testimonial, the more weight their letter of support will carry. An ideal letter of support would not only communicate enthusiasm about your nonprofit's work and lend credibility to your application but include some sort of commitment of resources. The exact nature of that support would obviously depend on the circumstances. A local business might offer a gift in kind. A donor might pledge a specific amount of money. A corporation might commit to giving staff some pro bono hours to spend on volunteering to help your nonprofit. The more evidence you can offer that the funder will not be alone in supporting your project or program, the better. This improves the likelihood that your proposal will be well received.

You may wish to include specific details about board members and staff. While this might feel odd, if there is significant relevant expertise to highlight here, then including biographies or even resumes for key personnel is completely appropriate. If you do not, nobody else is going to talk up your people. Teams are critical to execution; remember that your team's connection to the problem and deep understanding of it uniquely qualifies you to solve it. Consider what skills are most important for achieving the task at hand and draw a clear connection that establishes how each person will help accomplish it. What key competencies make them so impressive? What similar successes have they previously had? Paint a picture of a cohesive team coming together to deliver an essential project to benefit their community.

Finally, quality testimonials can potentially change the entire context of your grant proposal. There's nothing more compelling than feedback from the people your organization serves. A good testimonial tells a story of transformation. What was the person's original starting point, where did they end up, and how specifically did your project or program help? You may tidy up basic spelling and punctuation corrections but let your subject's authentic voice shine through without being filtered or polished. Telling your story through a human lens brings a diversity of voices that helps your proposal stand out even after the numbers have been forgotten.

Testimonials can be found all around you in the thank you notes your nonprofit receives, in emails, and in impromptu conversations. You can also recruit strong testimonials by asking specific questions in follow-up surveys, such as: What aspects of the program were most valuable for you, and why? If you do not get the types of responses you are looking for, do not hesitate to follow up and dig a little deeper. Testimonials are a powerful way to illustrate why your donors keep coming back and why your team is so committed to your mission.

MORE TEMPLATES AND SAMPLES TO GET YOU STARTED

Now that you have a clear picture of what goes into a proposal and how to approach the various sections of a grant application, here are some templates and samples to give you inspiration. Always give yourself plenty of time to work on each application. According to research from GrantStation (2019), developing a strategic plan and writing the grant application took up to five days each for 60% or more of respondents surveyed. Starting early and working on one component at a time will make the process smoother and result in a more compelling proposal overall.

Here is a general structure you can follow to format your grant application.

1. Proposal template

GRANT NAME:

DATE SUBMITTED:

SUBMITTED TO:

SUBMITTED BY:

I. PROJECT DESCRIPTION (*problem statement, goals and objectives, target population, project activities, key staff*)

____

____

____

____

____

II. SUCCESS CRITERIA (*measurable outcomes*)

____

____

____

____

____

III. ORGANIZATIONAL BACKGROUND

IV. CURRENT PROGRAMS, ACTIVITIES, AND ACCOMPLISHMENTS

V. GOALS & OBJECTIVES

VI. TIMELINE

____

____

____

____

VII. BUDGET

BUDGET PERIOD START AND END DATES

____

Income		Expenses	
Source	Amount	Use	Amount
Total		Total	
Net income			

LONG-TERM SOURCES / STRATEGIES FOR FUNDING

VIII. EVALUATION

---

2. Sample LOI

Jane Smith
Program Officer
Blue Sky Community Foundation
123 Hill Rd
Central City

Dear Ms. Smith:
Thank you for reading this letter of inquiry to your
Blue Sky Community Foundation. We hope to ascertain

your interest in receiving a full proposal for our Central City ABC Youth Latino Community Pilot Program. We respectfully request your consideration for a grant of $25,000.

This project represents an expansion of our current services and marks our first dedicated outreach effort to the burgeoning local Latino population. We plan to engage with them to drive uptake of our after-school programs, activities, and other related services.

Our pilot program lands squarely within your foundation's key areas of interest—at the intersection of investing in underprivileged young people to help them realize their full potential and providing essential community services and information to minority groups.

Our facility serves as a community hub for local youth and their families. Established in 2012, it now serves more than 60 young people each day. Our mission is to support them in achieving their best in academics, sports, and the arts.

Our latest surveys point to an extremely high satisfaction rate among youth and their parents of 97 percent. We provide nutritious snacks, educational tutoring, creative outlets, social opportunities, and physical exercise throughout the year.

The population of the neighborhoods we serve is expected to increase by 22 percent over the next two decades. Approximately 63 percent of them are projected to identify as Latino. Many of these families are at or below poverty level and have limited individual access to reliable transport. To help boost uptake of our after-school programs, we plan to begin offering optional transfer services, dropping off students at home after classes finish.

Our one-year pilot program objectives include:
1. *increasing the number of Latino students enrolled by 35%*
2. *recruiting 10 more volunteers to facilitate our after-school program*
3. *improving test scores among participating youth as measured at pre-set intervals throughout the year*

The total cost of our pilot program for one year is $50,000. Half of that has already been accounted for thanks to commitments from both the county government and other funders.

Your investment of $25,000 would cover the remainder of the funding needed to fully implement the pilot project. Our board of directors is eager to embark on this project, and we have received expressions of interest from volunteers.

We appreciate your consideration of this exciting project and look forward to hearing from you soon.

Sincerely,
Sarah Green
Executive Director
ABC Youth

3. Sample grant proposal

Cover letter
Alex Hill
Program Officer
Northern Foundation
123 Whitehall Rd
Central City

Dear Mr. Hill:
The JOY (Just Older Youth) Association is seeking a grant to provide support services to seniors in Eastern City. The elderly (65+) comprises 25% of the population

in this area. Retirees often struggle to adjust to life after work and declining health. Our work spans two complementary streams: organizing social outings and events for retirees and delivering meals to the homes of seniors with mobility restrictions.

Funding in the amount of $130,250 is requested to support the meal delivery program. The total cost of the meal delivery service for one year is $180,000, the rest of which will be covered by contributions from local businesses. Your investment would cover the outstanding balance required to deliver this project.

Our work aligns closely with your foundation's key priority: supporting and advocating for our senior citizens. Since our organization's inception, we have continued to expand our services engaging with an average of 4 percent more local seniors each year. We currently deliver regular meals to 170 local households. The recipients are seniors aged between 67 and 90 on fixed incomes with little or no family support.

The population of the neighborhoods we serve is projected to grow by 10 percent over the next decade. Due to the aging population at large and the amenities in this area, 72 percent of new arrivals are likely to be aged 65 or older. Many of these senior citizens live on their own.

Our objective for the next calendar year is to deliver meals to an additional 10 percent of local seniors, who can opt to receive deliveries on a daily, twice weekly, or weekly basis.

Thank you for your consideration of our proposal. We look forward to hearing from you soon.
Sincerely,
Alana White
Executive Director
Joy Association

Executive summary

The JOY Association in Eastern City is seeking a grant to expand our meal delivery program with the objective of ensuring all local seniors have adequate, nutritious food to eat while fostering a sense of community connection in the process. We intend to deliver meals to an additional 17-20 households in the calendar year ahead. Funding in the amount of $130,250 is requested to support this program.

Organization

The JOY Association was established in 2017 by a group of five seniors aged between 60 and 85. These empty nesters were neighbors who found themselves at a loss after major life transitions such as stopping work, becoming widowed, or having their families move away for jobs. Spearheaded by May Burke, they sought to organize activities and support services catering to the specific needs of seniors. We now serve 250 older adults each week with a variety of programs and services, including delivering regular meals to the homes of 170 seniors. Our mission is to help older people maintain a healthy, independent lifestyle and maintain their quality of life.

Our purpose is as follows:
1. *facilitate social interaction and community involvement*
2. *foster independence and dignity*
3. *break down common myths and stereotypes about aging*
4. *encourage living life to the fullest*

Our program director, Jennifer Reeves, has an extensive background in public service. She previously held a number of policy roles focused on retirement and the aging population. She is frequently quoted in the media as an expert in this area, most recently on Channel Five's morning show Breakfast and in M2 Woman magazine. Our coordinator, Shaun Freeman, began with us as a volunteer five years ago and has served in various capacities across our two main programs in that time. He was named a Local Hero in last year's National Volunteer award scheme.

Needs statement

Many older people in Eastern City struggle with the ever-increasing costs of living, including the costs of buying groceries. One in three recipients says their delivered meal is the main source of food for that day.

In addition, social isolation is a major issue. Most of our recipients feel disconnected from the fabric of society. They yearn for social interaction. They relish their independence and do not want to feel like a burden on their families but do not wish to enter assisted living. Many seniors can easily go for days without seeing other people. It is not uncommon for an older person who lives alone to fall, injure themselves, and be unable to call for help.

Overall, social isolation is associated with poor health, increased risk of dementia, and premature death. Our service can act as a lifeline in this regard.

Program description

We deliver fresh meals to recipients' homes either daily, twice a week, or once a week. Typical meals meet nutritional guidelines and can be tailored to suit dietary needs or preferences. Nine out of 10 recipients say this service helps them to live independently.

Our meal delivery service helps many elderly and disabled people maintain their independence and provides much needed regular social contact. Over half of recipients say their interaction with the person delivering their meal is the only social contact they have that day. Our delivery drivers often stop to chat, essentially conducting informal check-ins, which is especially important for recipients with more complex health issues.

They can help recipients address safety hazards in the home or assist them with any other essential tasks they may be struggling with on their own, such as changing light bulbs or managing laundry. The service has the potential to reduce the caring burden, giving peace of mind to family members who do not live close by and cannot regularly visit their loved ones.

Often recipients also form relationships with other meal recipients and wider Joy Association regular members.

"Since I've stopped working and my children moved to the other side of town, I've felt increasingly lonely without anything to fill my days. It's hard to get motivated to cook for one person. It's so nice to see a friendly face on my doorstep with a hot meal in hand to boot." - June, meal recipient

June's husband died many years ago and her remaining siblings live overseas or out of town. Her two sons recently moved away to be closer to their jobs and their own children's schools. She downsized to a smaller property in a nearby community and found herself without much of a support network. She developed a bond with the local volunteer who delivered her meals (initially weekly, now daily) and now regularly attends our social outings with other JOY members to croquet, arthouse films, botanic gardens, etc.

Goals and objectives

Our goal is to empower local seniors to live life to the fullest. This program supports older people to live independently in their own homes and age in place. The main objective of our meal delivery service is expanding our current base of recipients and maintaining or improving our 95% rating on satisfaction surveys.

Program budget

Supplies (mainly ingredients, including $23,890 in donations from local manufacturers and retailers) - $155,000

Packaging and other supplies/equipment - $9,000

Fuel costs - $5,000

Staff costs (including three volunteer delivery drivers) - $11,000

Total costs = $180,000

Overall, our organization is funded through private/foundation grants (51%), government grants (34%), corporate sponsorships (10%), and dona-tions/fundraising (5%). We have twice received funding through the central government's Age Concern Fund for our programs.

In the future, we plan to explore options to increase the sustainability of our operations, such as more recyclable or compostable packing, strategic use of frozen ingredi-ents for variety and convenience, or hosting shared meals at a community center to facilitate social inclu-sion. We already provide transfers for seniors on our social outings and could extend this service to encom-pass transport to shared meals.

We also intend to intensify our fundraising efforts and cultivate more individual donors. Additionally, one of our corporate supporters, Acme International, has expressed interest in sponsoring one of our delivery routes. Flamegrill, a restaurant situated next to the local Coles supermarket that provides us with many fresh and dry ingredients, has also offered the use of its facilities for cooking purposes once a week.

Evaluation

We track the number of meals delivered every week. This will be updated and reported each quarter to monitor growth. In addition, recipients are surveyed every six months to assess their satisfaction with the service. This is centrally managed by our coordinator. Delivery drivers dispense and collect the surveys when they visit each recipient at home. These are then analyzed by the coordinator and disseminated more widely.

STRATEGICALLY POSITIONING AND PITCHING YOUR NONPROFIT

Finally, it bears repeating that regardless of how worthy your project or program is, how you *position* your nonprofit has everything to do with your odds of success. If there's one thing I want you to take away from this, it's the importance of retaining a strategic mindset and pitching well.

Alignment matters. If you have the choice, pitch to an organization that is a natural fit and that will be excited about your project from the get-go. Building on a warm connection will only further increase your chances of success. Your proposal should clearly demonstrate how what you are doing fits in with the areas they already know well and prioritize. Speak their language and play up common interests. Remember that you have limited space to make your charitable cause memorable. The reality of the human attention span and memory is that both are limited. Trying to pack too much in and convey everything only results in the reader retaining nothing at all. If they come away only remembering one thing from your proposal, what should that be?

Foundations and nonprofits share a common goal—improving outcomes in the areas in which they operate. Although it can be difficult to quantify these goals, it's imperative to focus on performance measures and find a way to present your desired impact in a clear, measurable manner to funders. After all, many projects begin with great promise only to wind up with dashed hopes, limited impact, and uncertain prospects for the future. Remember that although you are asking for money, it doesn't mean they are above you. Consider yourselves as equals engaging in a dialog over a potential deal. Go in with the confidence to have a transparent conversation. Be honest about what stage you are at, what you have accomplished so far, and what you envision for the future. Your vision for the end game should be magnetic and infectious. Convey exactly why you are so driven to solve this problem and why you and your team are the ones to solve it.

As publicly traded organizations are increasingly held to account for their risks, nonprofits can benefit from applying a similar lens to their work and addressing this upfront in proposals. A few institutions are also beginning to look for this component in applications. They are naturally receptive to the role of risk management; it's in their best interests to ensure grant recipients are spending with a conservative approach. It's difficult to truly understand your priorities without a clear understanding of the risks faced across all areas, from governance and compliance to development, finances, operations, and reputation management. When putting a grant proposal together, consider organizational risk—in relation to funding, governance, and people—as well as strategic risk and executional risk.

To get a picture of the potential risks associated with your project, have everyone involved come together to conduct an initial risk inventory. Brainstorm all the possible risks that could pop up throughout its lifecycle. Rate the likelihood of each risk occurring, and quantify the impact it would have on time, cost, and quality. Then, you can devise mitigation strategies accordingly, so you can be honest about the risks and how you will deal with them in your proposal. Instead of worrying about exposing organizational weaknesses, show that you are aware of weak spots and articulate how you will strategically deploy to get the job done for maximum efficiency and effectiveness. An experienced program officer is always looking for red flags. The fact is, they must reject the majority of applications they receive. Do not give them an easy reason to turn yours down.

CHAPTER ACTIVITY: CREATE YOUR PROPOSAL TEMPLATE

Of all the activities in this chapter, this will prove to be the most demanding and time consuming but doing it well will be the most rewarding. Set aside some time and go to a place where you are undisturbed with a piece of paper or your laptop. In two hours or less, you want to create a detailed document with the following:

- Your organizational background – What is your nonprofit about? How did it come to exist? Where are you registered (give legal name and physical address)? How long have you been operational? What are some of your achievements? What is your philosophy? What typical programs do you run? Who benefits from your work? Who do you partner with?

- The problem you are solving – What gap have you seen? Why is your project/program needed? What evidence is there that the problem is real (research, anecdotal evidence, etc.)?

- How do you plan to solve it – What solutions do you have for the problem? Who is the target population for your solution?

- A project description with goals and objectives – Why exactly are you asking for money? Is it a new project or an existing one? How would it/does it work? Who is in charge? Who would benefit from it? What are your goals and objectives? Make sure your goals are S.M.A.R.T.

- Your operational strategy – How will you make your goals a reality? Give a logical and robust plan for achieving the goals for your project. What are the key activities?

- How you will assess success – How will you measure results? What will success look like?

- A timeline and a budget – How long do you think the project will last? How will you spend the money, if you receive it, and how much are you asking for?

It should take you about 15 minutes to work on each bullet point. The bullet points represent some major sections in a grant proposal. Paint with broad strokes at this point. Include as much detail as you can and try to have fun while doing so. It will help your cause to do this exercise at the time of the day when you are most productive. If you are stuck, use the questions provided as prompts and detail your answers. After answering these questions, you will have proposal template answers that are specific to your nonprofit and your project that you can always tweak to suit the funding opportunity you are applying for.

6

GETTING YOUR NONPROFIT TO STAND OUT FROM THE REST

The grant landscape is becoming increasingly competitive. You should always be thinking about the best way to get your proposals to stand out from the crowd in order to win funding. It's easy to get tunnel vision when you've been immersed in your cause for a long time. In this chapter, I will offer ten strategic tips for planning and writing a grant application that stands out. Knowing who you are and what you stand for will be key to successfully selling your story.

Tips to help your nonprofit stand out

1. Prep your toolkit

Be prepared. Compile all your collateral in one place so that it's ready for you to pull out when needed. Many grants are only open for a short window of time. Having this material handy will make it much easier to write out a fantastic grant application when you get the opportunity. You can then spend your time crafting the most effective proposal possible without worrying about digging up supporting content. It also pays to have a similar arsenal of potential projects that you can draw upon. If a funding opportunity arises, you can match one of these concepts to the grant. You want to avoid getting into the situation where you are scrambling to shape a project to fit the criteria for a grant as opposed to serving the needs of your community.

2. Keep your funder in mind as you write

The people who read, assess, and score your proposals are human too. Whether they are paid staff or volunteers, it is important to write your application with your reviewer in mind. Make it as easy as possible for them to understand. Assume that the reader has never heard of your nonprofit and knows nothing about the community you serve, the problem you are solving, what you do, or how you do it. This application is all they have to go on, so you need to spell out everything they need to know. Since they do not inhabit your world, reduce or cut out industry-specific terminology. Explain acronyms the first time they are mentioned and use plain language wherever possible.

3. Follow the instructions/templates

Most of the time, there will be an application form to complete and guidelines you are expected to follow. There may be specific questions you need to answer and attachments you need to include. Follow any instructions to the letter. Respond to questions in the order in which they are listed and echo the terminology they use. After all, if you cannot take directions at this stage, the logical assumption would be that you probably will not follow directions when it comes to delivering reports or other follow-up items after you are awarded a grant.

4. Leave enough time

As previously mentioned, you may not get much time to write a proposal. Build in enough time for input or edits from other stakeholders. Do not miss this step, as outside feedback can help you make a stronger case. Make a list of all documents that need to be submitted, key dates for completing and reviewing drafts, and any other tasks involved—along with who is responsible for each.

5. Focus on strengths

Any charity can rattle off a mile-long laundry list of what they need: a new building, another staff member, or more equipment. Unfortunately, these are not compelling arguments for a funder who is looking to support change. A grant giver wants to know about your solutions to community challenges and the impact of your work. Present your proposal as coming not from a needy nonprofit at risk of going under but a healthy, viable, and competitive organization worthy of investment. Think along the lines of crafting a pitch not a request. Focus on presenting your strengths well and how these strengths can help you achieve your project outcomes. Narrow it down to the most relevant and important points. You might have ten great reasons, but taken as a whole, this might diminish their impact. Boiling it down to three sharp, succinct points that convey your strengths, however, can make for a more powerful case.

6. Ensure you are involving the right stakeholders

As you design your project, be sure to involve the right people. A stakeholder group that is critical to creating impactful programs is the population you serve. However, they are often overlooked in the process. Their input can show you exactly what they are struggling with, why they are struggling with it, and what can be done to break the cycle. This will strengthen the story you have to tell through your applications. If you can point to ways that your target audience helped to co-design your initiatives, this will lend extra credibility to your proposal in the eyes of a funder.

7. Include partners where relevant

Many non-profit organizations collaborate with other groups or agencies to deliver their services. Funders want to see that you are teaming up with other partners to address the root cause of the problems you are tackling. Quality partnerships add credibility to your proposal rather than detract from it. Collaborations can maximize the use of grant funds through coordinating services to the target population in the most efficient way. Outline how you will share resources and what each partner brings to the table. What role will they play? Define their involvement and how much they will do. Specify the type of contributions involved whether it's personnel, facilities, expertise, equipment, or cash.

8. Present a comprehensive budget

A budget is not just a matrix of numbers. Your budget narrative should clearly show to the reader how you plan to leverage other funds to deliver your project and what cost-saving measures you will deploy. Demonstrate that you have thought about how you intend to capitalize on all available resources to make the most out of a funder's investment. In relation to partnerships, be sure to detail any cash contributions that will come into play, as well as non-monetary contributions—also known as *in-kind* contributions.

9. Study other successful grant applications

There is no better way to improve than to learn from those who have gone before you. Reading successful grant proposals will help you hone your own grant writing skills. There are some samples provided in the previous chapter and many more available online at websites like candid.org and thegrantadvantage.net. Do not copy them blindly but read through them and take note of what works. Find ways to apply these principles in your own grant applications. Find ways to tell your own story and refine your own voice.

10. Do not give up

Writing winning grants is a unique skill that can be developed. If you are willing to dedicate the time and effort to learning, you will get out as much as you put in. While your first few attempts may not bear fruit, reach out to the funder and ask for feedback about what might have made your application stronger. Use that information to enhance subsequent proposals.

CROSS CHECK EVERYTHING AGAINST YOUR MISSION STATEMENT

You are guaranteed to stand out if your proposal remains true to everything you stand for as a nonprofit. By virtue of where you are located, what you do, and how you do it, your nonprofit is already unique. If you align everything to your mission statement, it will increase your chances to get the funding significantly. A mission statement is an important part of any organization's identity. It captures a vision, purpose, and target audience and can convey a lot to a potential grant giver. Use the mission statement you clarified in Chapter 1 to guide you to position your nonprofit in a compelling way in your proposals.

In a well written mission statement, there is a balance stricken between its role in your organization's public image and its role in internal communications and strategy. The mission statement guides you and your staff in all that you do. It also makes outsiders want to learn more about your organization and get involved, thereby helping attract funding. A great mission statement rallies everyone involved around a common goal, adding clarity to your operations. Think of it as a compass or your North Star in terms of evaluating options and making decisions. It's impossible to prioritize everything, so your mission statement can help you focus on the right things. Mission statements will help your entire nonprofit act consistently as well as influence your organizational culture. Your staff and volunteers want to believe in the work they do.

Make sure that your mission statement distills the essence of your organization into one or two sentences. It should explain why your nonprofit exists, whom it serves, and how. You can edit it if you find it to be inaccurate. It needs to be unambiguous and memorable. Keep it concise, avoiding long or complex words or phrases, buzzwords, jargon, or generalities. Get specific, evoke emotions, and make it something that is easy to remember and repeat. To hone in on the value-add of your solutions, encourage participation from your working group. Collect insights and feedback from everyone you can: staff, board members, volunteers, partners, and supporters.

Powerfully written mission statements can help nonprofits stand out from the rest of the crowd. Take this one from Watts of Love: *Our mission is to bring people the power to raise themselves out of the darkness of poverty through solar lighting.* (Our Values - Watts of Love, 2021, Watts of Love). It inspires, communicates the organization's purpose, and clearly mentions the solution it offers. Alternatively, consider charity: water's mission statement: *charity: water is a non-profit organization bringing clean and safe drinking water to people in developing nations.* (About Us | charity: water, 2022, charity: water). It cuts to the chase touching on who the organization serves, where those people live, and what the organization actually does. In just a few words, it summarizes its purpose using terms anyone would understand. Finally, let's look at an example from First Descents: *First Descents provides life-changing, outdoor adventures for young adults impacted by cancer and other serious health conditions.* (Who We Are - First Descents, 2022, First Descents). In clearly specifying the age range served, this snappy mission statement is laser focused. The nonprofit's work is summed up with a compelling descriptor and packs a punch.

USE YOUR MISSION STATEMENT TO ENSURE ALIGNMENT

It is already clear so far that successfully winning grants rests on finding the right fit with similarly aligned grant givers. Clarity of purpose will help you sharpen your focus and narrow in on the most likely partners. Here are a few further tips for advancing your interests by prioritizing fit and building credibility to support your story. Double-check that your mission, objectives, and values truly align with the funder's. Something might seem like a good fit, but that does not mean it actually is. Closer inspection may yield some criteria that disqualify your nonprofit or reveal clashing values.

Compare the application deadline with the payout date. If the timelines do not match up with your project deadlines, then it simply is not the right grant to pursue at this time. Then, make sure that the funding available matches your project needs. If limits are not specified, do some further research; announcements of previous recipients can help you get a rough sense of the amounts typically awarded. How does that stack up against your projected costs? If you need $80,000 for a project, but the grantor has previously paid out an average of $3,000 per organization, it may not be the best fit. A grantmaker wants assurance that their funds will help you deliver your project, so you would need to explain where the rest of the funding would come from, outlining how this grant fits into your larger project funding strategy.

THE BOTTOM LINE: SELLING YOUR NONPROFIT'S STORY

Every charity has a story to tell about its organization and the impact of its work. As a grant writer, you need to believe in that story. If you have bought into it, you will be able to pitch it much more powerfully. While it is important to adhere to the rules when putting a proposal together, it is also essential to make sure your nonprofit's story comes across as well. Letting that unique voice and personality shine through will be crucial to convincing grantmakers to get on board. As a non-profit organization, your future hinges on your ability to secure outside funding, and the key to successful fundraising often lies in compelling storytelling.

All great stories have a setting, plot, strong characters, and satisfactory conclusion. Determine the main take-away of the story you want to tell beforehand. Then, begin with the who, where, and when of your nonprofit's origin story. Describe the setting; this is especially important when funders target a specific location. Lay out the problem or need and who it affects. Then, once you have established the obstacles, outline the desired outcome and the actions taken to reach the resolution.

When writing a grant, your natural inclination is usually to portray your nonprofit as the hero in your narrative. However, the real heroes are the people or population you serve. When crafting your project or program descriptions, instead think of your organization as their wise guide. Paint a picture of the problem or need faced by the hero and how, with your help, you can conquer that nemesis together. We instinctively connect with stories and become invested in seeing how a story arc plays out. The more captivating your narrative, the more likely you are to invigorate a reader into taking decisive action to support your cause. Take that problem and spin it into a narrative with a happy ending all around. You can try building a story around one of the individuals your project or program is helping. Describe their background, what their struggles are, and then how they will benefit specifically from the project. This will help make your grant proposal seem more real and impactful. Now, although they are not reflected directly in the story you have told so far, the funder will be a key character going forward. Consider their motivations and goals. Remind them that the story relies on them playing their part and make it clear how their contribution is going to make all the difference.

Inject passion into every facet of your proposal. Write with zest about your charity's founders and their driving purpose. Write with compassion about the problem you plan to solve using the grant funds. How can you bring to life the reality of what people are facing and the challenges they are juggling? Employ adjectives to convey the severity of the situation and use your needs statement to create tension. Likewise, use emotive language to illustrate the transformation and result.

When incorporating facts and figures, try to make use of tables and graphics, and contrast these with real-life scenarios. A case study showing how someone turned their life around as a result of your program is incredibly powerful. As the saying goes, a single death is a tragedy; a million deaths is a statistic. You do not need to try to cover every type of client you serve—just one or two relevant personas. If your nonprofit is young and your projects unproven, focus on your own staff and volunteers. Perhaps they have overcome their own hurdles and hardships and are now channeling that energy and focus for a greater good. You could also highlight how a key donor originally connected with your cause and has supported it ever since. Given word count restrictions, you may wonder how you are expected to fit all this into your application. Stories do not need to be lengthy. Even a few lines will suffice. Extract the juiciest, most colorful quotes and anecdotes that will land with the most impact.

When you boil it down, grant writing is a form of storytelling. Your story should convey the facts in a compelling manner, delivering an ultimately triumphant narrative that pays off for the reader and satisfies their need for a neat conclusion. Grant reviewers read a lot of proposals, so they gravitate towards those that are interesting and easy to read, as well as those that fit into the framework of what they are expecting to see. It is up to you to capture their attention, highlight how your work matches their priorities, and why that compatibility makes for a natural partnership.

CHAPTER ACTIVITY: PUT IT ALL TOGETHER AND CUSTOMIZE TO YOUR TOP PROSPECT

At this point, you have content for most sections of the proposal. The idea is to put them in the right format and to edit them to target the number one prospect you identified in Chapter four. Follow the format provided in the proposal sample in Chapter 5. Use the answers you have provided in Chapter 5 to fill out the relevant sections as follows:

- Your organizational background – organizational background
- The problem you are solving – needs/problem statement
- How you plan to solve it – program goals and objectives

- A project description with goals and objectives – project description
- Your operational strategy – methods and strategy
- How you will assess success – evaluation plan
- A timeline and a budget – budget and sustainability

Do not worry about sections like the cover letter and the executive summary that you do not have yet. Simply fill out these sections and edit them to fit in with the prospect you will be sending the proposal to. Use the keywords they have used in their guidelines as much as is realistically possible. Highlight the places where your goals and missions align and make the proposal as compelling as you can. At this point, you can also create a story representing the typical person you help and add it to sections of your proposal, more so in the organizational background, problem you are solving, your strategy, and evaluation plan.

7

INSPIRATION FROM FUNDING INNOVATION

Like venture capital firms, foundations and other grantmakers only fund a small percentage of the funding requests they receive. Venture capitalists typically have a significant impact on the start-ups they invest in, supporting the long-term growth of those companies. However, grant givers parcel out much smaller amounts to higher numbers of recipients over much shorter periods of time. Grants only cover a small portion of any nonprofit's expenses. That is why you need to get creative in your approach to fundraising.

It is time to start thinking beyond conventional grant giving. This chapter will delve into best practices and trends in the world of nonprofit funding. You will come away with fresh inspiration from innovation in philanthropic funding that you can apply to your own fundraising efforts. You will also find some additional resources to help with continuously sharpening up your grant writing at the end of this chapter.

GET INNOVATIVE IN YOUR OUTREACH

As a non-profit organization, much of your success hinges on connection with the community you serve and staying relevant. Prioritize getting active in your local area to build up brand recognition and to get to know the people who could well be your best supporters and advocates. Participate in local events like festivals and markets to get in front of potential donors and volunteers as well as people who may potentially benefit from your programs and services. A physical presence at a booth or stand provides a face for your nonprofit and will help raise awareness of your mission. If possible, try to mobilize a group of ambassadors to go out and engage with the public on a regular basis.

The work of a non-profit professional never ends. Building and cultivating relationships within your community will be an ongoing process. Consider hosting training events and seminars, which give your team an opportunity to practice their pitches and teach about what they know best. Sharing expertise will provide extra value to those who attend and help to promote your nonprofit in the process. These could even be held virtually. Think outside the box. Along with educational or professional development workshops and webinars, this could extend to art classes, performances, and shows. All of this helps to raise your organizational profile and cement what you are known for. The stronger your reputation, the stronger your grant applications will be.

ASK FOR MORE THAN MONEY

Cash is king, which is why fundraising usually takes up so much of a typical nonprofit's time and energy. But that is not to say it's the only thing your organization needs. Many nonprofits would benefit equally from non-monetary support such as hands-on help in molding strategies, prototyping new ideas, and building their systems and capability. Your grant applications can reflect the full scope of your needs if you know that the funding agency can help you potentially meet those.

In the venture capital world, funders often take a seat on the board of the companies they fund. This is less common in nonprofits, not least due to potential conflicts of interest and time constraints. That said, it is not entirely unheard of. According to Deloitte (2015), Draper Richards Kaplan Foundation, a global venture philanthropy firm, supports grantees' success by taking a seat on the board for three years. Precedent can also be seen in the case of New Profit—a funder of innovative nonprofits serving low-income Americans that operates much like a sophisticated venture capital firm. According to the Harvard Business Review (2010), New Profit performs rigorous analysis on potential recipients and actively manages its investments to increase their social impact. A partner serves on each nonprofit's board and becomes a day-to-day adviser helping the leadership team with everything from recruiting to refining its social change model. New Profit also helps the nonprofits in its portfolio develop measurement frameworks for impact and organizational performance and provides them with access to high-level strategic advisers. These advisers coach on strategy development and growth planning.

At a nonprofit where leaders are head-down working to create impact, core organizational functions are often underdeveloped. Funders can support organizations in building these skills, thus playing a more active role in their ultimate success. This could look like connecting a nonprofit to critical mentorship, training, and coaching opportunities. It could mean introducing them to other funders, influencers, media, and specialized professionals like accountants and lawyers. It could mean supporting outreach efforts, strategic planning, financial modeling, and communications strategy to shape public perceptions. Define whatever gaps you see in the skill sets of your team or strategy that currently weaken your nonprofit's resilience. Then you can hone in on how funders may be able to support you on remedying those, and which funders in particular may be best placed to help in that regard.

PRESENT HOW YOU ARE LEARNING AND IMPROVING

Implementing lasting change can often take years, if not decades. After taking a stake, investors typically engage with a start-up for as many as 10 years. Foundations work on a much shorter horizon. The typical timeframe of a grant leaves little time for recipients to come up with innovative programs or campaigns. However, you can play up the benefits of continuous learning and improvement for both funders and the wider system you operate within. Innovations often follow a long and winding path and accrue interesting smaller breakthroughs along the way that others in the field can leverage.

Social innovation is inherently risky. It is only through experimenting that new concepts can be tested and eventually proven. Trial and error yields constant learning. The nonprofit world could take a cue here from the world of entrepreneurship by embracing the principles of fast failure and radical transparency. Making our streams of successes and failures alike more public and creating a discourse around dissecting these lessons will benefit society as a whole. We can learn from what works and what does not only if failure is analyzed and shared widely. According to the European Venture Philanthropy Association (2015), this is why an increasing number of organizations are advocating for more openness in sharing stories of failures. The Canadian NGO Engineers Without Borders publishes an annual Failure Report (2017 Failure Report, 2017, Engineers Without Borders) in which engineers share their stories of failing and the lessons they learned as a result. This level of transparency—outlining what went wrong and why—benefits not just others in the organization, but those outside of it too.

Donors view nonprofits as the most likely organizations to develop solutions and instigate change but not always in isolation. A Fidelity (2016) study found that donors believe multiple groups have the best potential to find ways to overcome society's problems. They increasingly see both nonprofits and public-private partnerships as the most probable candidates to successfully address challenges. The idea of cross-sector collaboration, taking a broad view of stakeholders, is gaining traction. No single sector is charged with sole responsibility. It may be time to explore forming new partnerships with outside groups. For example, more and more universities are home to social change incubators, and businesses are increasingly building their social responsibility teams and capability. Non-traditional groups that are newer to the social sector have a particular opportunity to expand their reach and redefine their missions in the name of social impact.

To sustain organizational growth, you will need to look beyond the current round of funding. Consider proposing that a funder stays on board until your nonprofit is ready for the next stage of funding. According to the Harvard Business Review (1997), one organization that has successfully taken this approach is Cooperative Home Care Associates (CHCA). This New York-based, worker-owned cooperative provides health care to the elderly in their homes. When CHCA wanted to build on its success and expand its operations by launching a training institute, it approached a previous funder with a long-term plan for building self-sustaining cooperatives. That funder—the Charles Stewart Mott Foundation—then awarded CHCA a series of renewable grants over a seven-year period. Programs like this provide an incentive for funders to move away from the standard terms of just one or two years and toward longer-term periods where their grants can have more sustained impact. Meanwhile, another nonprofit, Family Service America, found success in pitching for funding for capacity building. Instead of proposing a new program, the organization laid out an analysis of its organizational needs. These ranged from recruiting and training to benchmarking and change management. Family Service America successfully convinced foundations to invest in strengthening its organizational capability as a way of driving program outcomes. (Virtuous Capital: What Foundations Can Learn from Venture Capitalists, 1997, Harvard Business Review).

GO BIG

Ask for too little in a grant application, and the funder may feel they could have more impact if they chose to fund a larger project instead. Think about the scale of your impact. Take a step back and look at the bigger picture while considering the context of the wider field you work within. When you see the whole landscape, what is missing? Which areas could you expand into? Finding powerful ideas with the potential to create lasting change requires you to do things differently from how you have always done them. It calls for exploring beyond the usual suspects to come up with new solutions. As you build a list of exciting opportunities, you should then prioritize these based on their potential for transformation. Try ranking each one according to the likely future impact it would have. Size matters when it comes to making a substantive impact on pervasive and complex societal problems. If there is one area where there's no excuse for thinking small, it's fundraising.

Regardless of the size of your nonprofit, the cause you are fighting for is an important one. Make sure you give yourself appropriate credit for that.

Thinking big could mean launching an ambitious new program or campaign. It might mean going for new funding streams. It might even mean coming up with an innovative new growth strategy. As described in a Stanford Social Innovation Review (2007) article, nonprofits that achieve the most growth invest in talent and build structures that support a high-growth model. For instance, housing nonprofit Help USA created a team of more than 30 people to apply for and manage complicated government contracts. The Oregon Food Bank built a $10 million distribution center with the ability to handle both fresh and frozen food, dramatically expanding the range of donations it was able to accept (How non-profits get really big, 2007, Stanford Social Innovation Review). These are just a few examples of thinking differently and expanding your horizons.

FURTHER RESOURCES

If you want to learn from the pros, there is plenty of advice available out there. Institutions and universities alike provide grant writing advice that can be freely accessed online. For starters, some general resources can be found at The Writing Center website by the University of North Carolina. For more rigorous training, you may like to investigate courses or workshops, such as Effective Grant Proposal Writing from the University of Notre Dame. For further tips and tools from official sources, visit the US Government grants website or the Environmental Protection Agency web page on grants.

CHAPTER ACTIVITY: WRITE YOUR COVER LETTER AND EXECUTIVE SUMMARY

So far, you have a near complete proposal already customized to your top prospect. It is now time to write your executive summary and cover letter. If time has passed between your working on the previous chapter and now, go through all sections of your proposal before writing your executive summary. The executive summary is meant to provide a brief overview of everything included in your proposal. You are generally asking yourself this question: *What is the essential problem you are solving with this work?*

Be sure to frame the need or problem as a succinct query before shifting into providing the answer through your proposed project or program. What do you intend to do? How will you do it? Why is this work so important? What has already been done? Provide a brief overview of the entire proposal including the amount of grant funding you are requesting. Then, write your cover letter following the guidelines provided in Chapter 5.

STAGE 3

REVIEWING YOUR PROPOSAL FOR COMMON PITFALLS

8

WHY DO GRANT PROPOSALS GET REJECTED?

You send off your grant proposal and wait patiently. The days, weeks, and months pass. Eventually, you receive a response—a generic "Thank you, but..." Immediately, you enter into a tailspin and begin second-guessing everything you did. Where did you go wrong? What else could you have included? After all those hours spent crossing *t's* and dotting *i's,* this is a real blow.

Getting an impersonal rejection with no reasons or suggestions invariably stings. However, funders rarely provide justification for denying your request. Numbers-wise, they are forced to turn down the majority of proposals that land on their desk. It takes a lot of resources to review all those applications; they simply may not have the time or people power to respond personally to each applicant. However, there are some common reasons that cause grantmakers to reject applications. Let's examine these in more detail and wrap up with some pointers on building credibility for your nonprofit to improve your chances next time around.

MISALIGNED GOALS

This is by far the main reason most funding requests are unsuccessful. If your nonprofit's goals do not match up with the funder's goals from the very start, then your proposal will not be in the running for long. Just like your organization, a foundation, government agency, or corporation will have a particular focus when it comes to projects it chooses to fund. Ideally, there should be an obvious relationship between your project or nonprofit and the priorities of the funder you apply to. That might be synergy in terms of target population, location served, or the type of service or program being provided.

Think back and ask yourself whether you fully understood the priorities of the funding agency. On the surface, it might have seemed like your organizations shared a similar vision and were both headed in the same direction. However, perhaps the more granular objectives of your proposal were not exactly in line with their specific goals. Consider the funder's vision, mission statement, values, and the inferred outcomes of those guiding principles. It may be the case that upon closer inspection, your goals were not as closely aligned as you imagined, or perhaps your application did not highlight the relevant connections clearly enough for the reader.

YOUR NONPROFIT DID NOT SEEM READY FOR FUNDING

Another reason grant applications frequently fail comes down to organizational readiness. In other words, your organization is not ready for funding or does not appear to be ready for it. Perception is as important as reality. Start by examining your nonprofit's structure. Is it a trust, association, or corporation? Who are the key players at the top level? Do they each fill a specific role in which they have particular expertise, or are some covering multiple functions? Ideally, your leadership team should be diverse, and each member should bring a track record of success in their respective areas. Any organizational audits should be carried out by wholly independent and respected firms. Being able to demonstrate efficiency will also elevate perceptions of your organizational readiness. Some grant givers will evaluate the percentage of total expenses going toward program costs. The majority—ideally 75% and up—of your organization's expenditure should be directed toward the delivery of your programs or services.

In addition to having your financial house in good order, funders expect to see clear goals, activities, and measures. Do your vision, mission statement, and goals reflect the maturity level of your nonprofit? Are these supported by robust evidence of needs or gaps in this area? Competency and capacity to execute also go hand in hand with organizational readiness. Are your staff members capable of implementing the work outlined by your grant application and prepared to execute? Do they have the necessary skills to evaluate and document the outcomes that need to be tracked? What about managing ongoing communications and compiling regular reports?

NON-MEASURABLE PROGRAM OBJECTIVES

High on the list of common reasons for rejection is a lack of clearly articulated objectives. Have you used realistic, definitive objectives? Recall that objectives are tangible subsets of often intangible goals. Ill-defined or hard to measure objectives can be a death knell for any grant proposal. A grantmaker is naturally going to assess your plan of action in relation to the desired outcomes. It is important to determine how you will quantify the impact of your project or program. You will then need to explain the exact steps required to achieve those objectives in your application.

A WEAK BUDGET

The financial section of your grant proposal must be able to withstand scrutiny. Any anomalies will stand out to the eye of a seasoned reviewer. Grant givers are financially savvy and can quickly spot problems or inconsistencies in a proposed budget from a mile off. Be realistic and transparent with every line item. Areas like staffing or consultant costs will usually be the most closely examined. You can also expect that funders will be looking for any estimates that you may have taken liberties with, so aim for the highest degree of accuracy possible. If you do not have complete confidence in your budget, neither will an outsider.

NOT FOLLOWING INSTRUCTIONS TO THE LETTER

Most grant givers supply guidelines, if not specific instructions and templates, as to how they want applications presented. For one thing, standardized proposals are easier to review. For another, this minimizes the number of applicants blasting out a one-size-fits-all application. It also helps to weed out any nonprofits that do not follow the provided instructions. Simply ensuring you adhere to the guidelines and meet the application deadline is a non-negotiable first step.

Otherwise, you will not make it to the next round for consideration. Follow the structure and format as outlined down to the smallest details. Resist the urge to include a host of supporting documentation simply because you believe it might help your chances of securing the grant.

A POORLY WRITTEN APPLICATION

If you approach grant writing with the mindset that a proposal is the equivalent of a prospectus designed to attract like-minded people to invest in your organization, you will have a head start. A grant application is your best chance to make a good impression. Make it easy to read. Write in an accessible manner that can be understood by anyone, even someone unfamiliar with your sector. Write in specifics and focus on tangible concepts wherever possible. If it takes a reviewer too long to figure out what you are trying to say, they will likely lose interest and move on to the next one. Keep your writing concise. While it may be tempting to try and pack in more detail, this will not work in your favor. Finally, any sloppy writing will obviously count against you. Proofread your work thoroughly and ask a third party to read it through with fresh eyes to ensure your proposal is polished to a high standard.

LACK OF CREDIBILITY

Nonprofits also fail to win grants because of a lack of credibility. This is especially true when you are starting out and angling for your first grant or first big donor. Grantmaking agencies want to know that their funds are being distributed to trustworthy nonprofits with integrity. You know that your mission is worthy and that your entire team takes it very seriously. You also need a track record in order to be considered credible by outside funders. One way to combat this perceived weakness is to partner with other reputable organizations that are more established, essentially piggybacking off their name by association. However, your nonprofit will also need to build its own credibility by reducing information asymmetry and cultivating an image that evokes trust.

You should aim to develop a solid communications and engagement strategy to build visibility and engender trust with your community, donors, and media. Unlike advertising, public relations is about reaching out to media and influencers to build your presence without paying for coverage. As your nonprofit's name begins to appear in more and more outlets, this will enhance trust and goodwill on the part of donors—often resulting in an increase in donations.

Using media to build credibility for your brand can have an immediate impact if you can land a mention in a mainstream publication. The media loves a feel-good story. Sometimes they may approach you, but more often than not, it will be up to you to let them know about what your organization is up to. As with engaging early with potential funders, it is worth taking a similar approach to engaging journalists. Do some research to ensure you are contacting the right reporters. You could compile a list of reporters who cover stories in your area or in your industry and follow them on Twitter or LinkedIn. Reshare or comment on their posts and follow up by pitching them a story about your cause. You must present an interesting and timely angle in order to capture their attention.

Consider where your target audience spends their time and what media they consume. The best way to reach people and get the word out about your mission is to show up where they already are. Consider reaching out to podcast hosts about setting up an interview; they are often looking for interesting guests to feature and have a dedicated audience soaking up every episode. There are a surprising number of existing podcasts in the nonprofit space. You are bound to find a few candidates. You can also reach out to relevant websites and blogs and propose writing a guest post for them. While this will obviously give you more exposure to their audience and increased brand visibility through SEO, they also stand to benefit through gaining fresh content to publish. When crafting your pitch, explain why you are approaching them specifically and how this blog post will provide value to their readers.

As with any partnership, collaborations work best when there is clear synergy between both parties' missions. For example, Mothers Against Drunk Driving partnered with Uber. Consider teaming up with other organizations or corporations to leverage their audience, customer base, or workforce. This gets your name and work in front of a new group of people. You might ask a local restaurant to donate a percentage of one day's sales to your cause or organize a raffle with a local sports team. In return, you would encourage your nonprofit's supporters to show up and spend their money there. Many workplaces are happy to support local charity projects through sponsorship, in-kind donations, and volunteer hours. This goes for local, in-person events too. Establish a presence at cultural and holiday celebrations, markets, or any other relevant events that draw crowds. You can contact event organizers and ask what role your organization could play on the day or what support you can provide.

Spend some time building your nonprofit's online presence by growing and nurturing a following on social media. The viral nature of social networks means that the more traction your content gets, the more momentum you build overall. You can also use relevant hashtags to make your content easier to discover. Be strategic in your approach and plan out what kind of content you will share, how often, and on which platforms. For example, along with sharing content about your programs and services, you can share more about each of your staff members, your organizational history, industry trends, and even amplify what your partners and sponsors are sharing on their own channels. Make the most of the visual nature of Facebook, Instagram, Pinterest, TikTok, etc. Share videos and images as much as possible. Give fans a reason to follow you. Respond to their comments, encourage tagging, and do not be afraid to use humor—people are seeking to be entertained on social media.

Finally, putting out your own content also serves to build your organization's credibility. Webinars and blog posts can then be easily repurposed into all manner of formats: syndicated to other publications, turned into info-graphics or SlideShare presentations, adapted into a LinkedIn column, or posted on social media. Do not try to reinvent the wheel every time. Take what you have and get more mileage out of it by molding it to suit other purposes. You should be able to reuse every piece of content in at least one other channel—one way or another.

CHAPTER ACTIVITY: REVIEW YOUR PROPOSAL AND RUN IT BY YOUR WORKING GROUP

Take time to go through your proposal to see if you have avoided the pitfalls discussed in this chapter.

- Do your goals align with your funders'? Read through their requirements one last time as you check your proposal.
- Are the goals of your project measurable?
- Is your proposal as detailed as it should be, with everything in the right place?
- Is your budget tight and reasonable?
- Have you established your credibility? Have you listed any partnerships you may have?

Have your working group go through the proposal and give feedback for each section. You can send them a list of things to look for as they review your proposal so that they catch anything that you may have missed. As they provide feedback, check your proposal against the cheat sheet in Chapter 9 as well.

9

YOUR CHECKLIST CHEAT SHEET

Now it is time for one final run through. Before you hit the submit button, you should always cross check proposals to make sure they hit the mark and embody all the characteristics of successful grant applications. Take a moment to review your proposal against this checklist. How many of these boxes does your grant application tick?

- **Contains SMART objectives in your project description**

What exactly will your project have achieved at the end of the grant period? What might the wider impact be beyond the immediate target audience? The broader the significance of the work, the better. It is also vital to tie your project objectives back to the priorities and goals of the funder. Always articulate project objectives using the SMART framework. They should be specific, measurable, achievable, realistic, and timely.

- **Clear, concise, compelling writing**

At the macro level, ensure you have clearly articulated your organization's mission, track record, goals, projected impact, and work plan. Ensure you have provided relevant details in each section and answered the key question. Incorporate a blend of statistics and anecdotes to bring the issue to life. When done right, a reader should come away eager to act on your proposed idea

Format your proposal so that it is easy to read. Break up dense text with subheadings, paragraphs, bullet points, boxes, figures, and diagrams. Lastly, ensure you do not exceed the word limit.

- **A powerful evaluation section**

The impact evaluation section of your grant proposal should outline how you will measure outcomes, why you have selected that particular method, who is responsible for tracking these metrics, what tools they will use, and when they will do so. This does not automatically require external evaluators or the use of new tools or methods. Consider how your nonprofit currently collects and analyzes data. There is no need to reinvent the wheel unnecessarily.

- **A well-crafted, thoughtful submission that has been reviewed by a colleague**

There is no excuse for cutting corners and dashing off a hastily put-together application. Take care to present information in a logical fashion, including facts and numbers that support a thorough and compelling proposal. Your work plan should address specific activities, accountability, timelines, and partnerships.

While it may read well to you, you are too close to the work to conduct the final review. Your brain and eyes start to read what should be there, rather than what is actually there. That is why you need an outsider to read through your submission well before the deadline. Enlist a trusted colleague to give feedback on your proposal, not only in terms of spelling and grammar, but to check whether your overall writing style is succinct and compelling. You may find that they spot gaps in the supporting details where you have not thoroughly answered the question at hand.

- **Shows passion specific to the topic/field**

Passion is an essential ingredient in any grant proposal. Your nonprofit's mission and story come into play here. Do not be afraid to highlight the origin story that led to its founding. A strong "why" is what keeps charitable causes going despite the many challenges they face. In your grant proposal, focus on opportunities, rather than hurdles or problems. Stress the unique qualities of your project and organization, while demonstrating a broad knowledge of similar initiatives in the wider sector.

- **Builds on your organization's track record**

Your grant application should place your proposed project or program within the overall context of your nonprofit's mission. Craft a punchy cover letter that presents an overview of your organization and your project, and relevant background material to support this narrative. It is crucial to present your nonprofit's history in the best possible light, showing how it is qualified to deliver the work ahead. Pointing to your established track record of success will give a funder confidence in your capacity to continue in the same vein. If your nonprofit is young and lacking sufficient experience in the field, play up other evidence of its credibility, such as media coverage and partnerships with established organizations.

If you have made it this far, congratulations! You are officially ready to send your grant proposal and take the next step toward winning more funding for your non-profit organization—preparing other proposals. All you need to do is clean it up and submit it to your top prospect.

CHAPTER ACTIVITY: CLEAN IT UP, PACKAGE IT AND HIT SEND

Give your proposal to a colleague you trust or perform the final clean up yourself. If you choose to do it yourself, give yourself a day or two to step away from the proposal and do other things. That way, when you come back to it, you will see it with fresh eyes. Check to see that the message is as clear as possible and evaluate the effect it is likely to have on the reader. Is the effect what you desired? Is your purpose clear? Is there irrelevant information? Are the ideas clear? Are your data/examples accurate? Is the tone appropriate for your audience? Is the length optimal?

Edit the structure as well. Does the proposal look appealing? See if the structure is organized; ensure that ideas flow logically and each section is at the right place. Is there a clear executive summary? Are there enough paragraphs? Does each paragraph have a clear topic sentence? Have you linked the sentences well? Make sure that the language you use is grammatically correct and remember to spell check. Use appropriate vocabulary and punctuation. Grammarly is very helpful with this—editing and proofreading.

The final thing to check for at this stage is the formatting. Good writing includes high readability. Does your final product look good? What font have you chosen? Have you highlighted important ideas? Is the formatting consistent? If you have done the previous steps well, this last one should take you ten minutes or less depending on the length of your proposal. You normally review to make sure that your content reads well and that the final draft has the intended effect on the reader. If possible, read parts of your writing aloud and listen to how they sound.

Remember that part of cleaning up your grant proposal is attaching any required additional documents. Add an appendices section with your budget and any extra material that makes it easier for the funder to understand your situation and appreciate your solution. Where possible, use charts and tables to illustrate ideas rather than simply describing them with words alone. Once you have done all this, your proposal is ready to be submitted. Submit it through the proper channels. All the best with your proposal!

FINAL THOUGHTS

If your nonprofit is in a tight spot and looking to raise funds quickly, grants are unlikely to be the silver bullet for your organization. However, they are a great solution for charities seeking funds to deliver pre-planned programs and should make up part of your long-term revenue strategy. Nonprofits must maintain diverse streams of income to reduce risk and ensure sustainability. Grant funding can play a key role in funding growth and launching new programs that otherwise wouldn't be possible. Receiving a grant from a well-respected foundation or government agency can also boost your organization's credibility. This in turn can help you land even more funding from other sources going forward. There are billions of dollars' worth of grants out there offered by foundations, government agencies, corporations, and other grantmakers. According to Grant Station (2019), the median largest individual award for grant seekers that year was $69,100. There are grants available for all kinds and sizes of nonprofits, and while many are designed to fund specific projects, there are also plenty that will help to cover operating expenses or capital costs.

That said, this money is not just sitting around waiting to be claimed. You will need to put in the work to ensure you meet the criteria and craft a compelling case for why your nonprofit deserves to receive its share of the pot. It does not end there, either—once funds are awarded, it is up to you to deliver on what was promised and report back on the impact of your project or program.

Remember that every grant-giving organization will have different requirements. Your success hinges largely on finding a suitable match and then crafting a narrative that connects with those values and pitches your nonprofit as a natural partner. No matter how powerful your nonprofit's mission, if you cannot tell a compelling story that weaves together its vision and impact, you will struggle to win attention and funding. The most successful grant recipients understand this and apply these core principles to every application sent out.

Developing grant writing skills is an invaluable asset for any nonprofit professional. Once you know how to write and win grant proposals, this can become a dependable source of revenue. Fortunately, following some best practices for writing grant proposals will set you ahead of the pack from the get-go.

By now, you should have a firm grasp of nonprofit grants, how to find potential opportunities, and how to engage with a funder early on to improve your chances of success. Throughout this book, I have walked you through the steps involved in writing an irresistible grant application—breaking down the elements of a proposal with specific examples and providing activities for you to do toward finishing a grant proposal. Finally, I outlined some common mistakes that frequently result in rejection and provided a cheat sheet to check your proposal against. You can refer back to that section before sending off each application to ensure it stands out and avoids the most common pitfalls that plague grant writers.

My vision in writing this book was to alleviate any apprehension you may feel in relation to grant writing and equip you with the confidence and insider knowledge to succeed. Now that you have the tools, go forth and win your next proposal.

Thank you for delving into the first part of *Nonprofit Fundraising Mastery 2-in-1 Collection*. Your thoughts and experiences matter to me. I kindly ask that, if you found this part valuable, please consider leaving a review for the entire collection on Amazon or Audible. Your insights not only support me in delivering better content but also aid fellow readers in their quest for quality resources.

REFERENCES

Bridgespan. (2011.) Donors want more information on impact. https://www.bridgespan.org/insights/blog/measuring-to-improve/blog-donors-want-more-information-on-impact

Candid. (2020.) Key facts on U.S. non-profits and foundations. https://www.issuelab.org/resources/36381/36381.pdf

Charity: water. (2022.) About Us | charity: water.https://www.charitywater.org/uk/about

Deloitte. (2015.) Case studies in funding innovation. https://www2.deloitte.com/content/dam/insights/us/articles/case-studies-in-funding-innovation-gates-foundation-grand-challenges-explorations/Funding-innovation_ENTIRE-ARTICLE_vFINAL_10_15_15.pdf

Engineers Without Borders. (2017.) 2017 Failure Report. https://www.ewb.ca/wp-content/uploads/2018/08/EWB_FAILURE-REPORT_EN_03-08-2018-pages.pdf

European Venture Philanthropy Association. (2015.) Learning from failures in venture philanthropy and social investment. https://evpa.eu.com/uploads/publications/Learning-from-failures_EVPA_2015report.pdf

Fidelity. (2016.) The future of philanthropy. https://www.fidelitycharitable.org/content/dam/fc-public/docs/insights/the-future-of-philanthropy.pdf

Fidelity. (2017.) Fidelity charitable study finds 64% of donors want to give more to charity, concerned about personal finances and impact. https://www.fidelitycharitable.org/about-us/news/study-finds-64-percent-of-donors-want-to-give-more.html

First Descents. (2022.) Who We Are - First Descents. https://firstdescents.org/who-we-are/

Foundation Center. (2004.) Foundation growth and giving estimates, 2004 preview. https://www.issuelab.org/resources/24885/24885.pdf

GrantStation. (2019.) The 2019 state of grantseeking report. https://grantstation.com/sites/default/files/2019-05/The%202019%20State%20of%20Grantseeking%20Report_0.pdf

Harvard Business Review. (2010.) The emerging capital market for non-profits. https://hbr.org/2010/10/the-emerging-capital-market-for-nonprofits

Harvard Business Review. (1997.) Virtuous capital: what foundations can learn from venture capitalists. https://hbr.org/1997/03/virtuous-capital-what-foundations-can-learn-from-venture-capitalists

King, Bernard J. (2011.) Poverty and literacy development: challenges for global educators. https://core.ac.uk/download/pdf/11049014.pdf

National Philanthropic Trust. Charitable giving statistics. https://www.nptrust.org/philanthropic-resources/charitable-giving-statistics/ and https://www.nptuk.org/philanthropic-resources/uk-charitable-giving-statistics/

New York Times. (2012.) Getting into a benefactor's head. https://www.nytimes.com/2012/11/09/giving/understanding-donor-behavior-to-increase-contributions.html

OECD. (2013.) England & Northern Ireland (UK) – Country Note –Survey of AdultSkills first results. https://www.oecd.org/skills/piaac/Country%20note%20-%20United%20Kingdom.pdf

Stanford Social Innovation Review. (2007.) How non-profits get really big. https://ssir.org/articles/entry/how_non-profits_get_really_big#

Submittable. (2020.) 34 grant statistics for 2020. https://blog.submittable.com/grant-statistics/

The Annie E. Casey Foundation. (2004.) Moving youth from risk to opportunity. https://files.eric.ed.gov/fulltext/ED485937.pdf

The Guardian. (2015.) Proving your impact: what funders want from charities. https://www.theguardian.com/society-professionals/2015/nov/04/impact-funders-charities-foundations-measurement

Watts of Love. (2021.) Our Values - Watts of Love. https://www.wattsoflove.org/about/our-values

NONPROFIT FUNDRAISING STRATEGIES

7 STRATEGIES TO CONSISTENTLY SECURE FUNDING AND ENSURE YOUR ORGANIZATION DOESN'T FAIL – USING GRANTS, GIFTS, DIGITAL, AND MORE . . .

JAMES RUELL

INTRODUCTION

"Fundraising is the gentle art of teaching the joy of giving."

— HANK ROSSO

You're exhausted, frustrated, and stressed. After years of leading a nonprofit, your go-to fundraising tactics just aren't bringing in as much as they used to—and nowhere near what your operating costs call for. The main question that weighs on your mind, and your small team, grows increasingly urgent with each passing day: How do we bring in more donations to stay afloat? You're a tight-knit group who toil tirelessly in service of the mission. When the essence of your goals and intentions is this pure—to help your local community—should just staying open one more day really be what you're worrying about? Unfortunately, it is.

Nonetheless, you're constantly overworked and overwhelmed by fundraising. The regular calendar of events requires a grueling amount of late-night and weekend work to organize, manage, and plan. And even before the onset of the pandemic—which sent demand for your services skyrocketing—income from the usual campaigns had already been on a slow but steady decline. The fundraisers you've relied on for years just aren't bringing in as much money as they used to. Surely there's a better way . . .

Sound familiar? I've experienced this, and there is a better way. The cycle of fundraising stress and being overwhelmed, while common—no wonder so many wind up leaving the sector altogether—doesn't need to be a certainty. There are easier, better ways to fundraise—and you don't need to scour the web to piece together random techniques to experiment with. Instead, from years of research and practice, I've pulled them all together in one book that you can reference time and time again. You'll learn the foundational best practices that I've learned from personal experience and that every fundraiser needs to know, as well as practical action steps that will start bringing money in the door.

How do I know what works? How can I help you with this? While we may never cross paths in real life, I know very well the hardship you face when it comes to fundraising. If we have never met before, it's a pleasure to meet you. I feel honored that you have picked up my book and I will do my best to pay you back for your trust. If every person who reads this book is able to raise just a little bit more money for their nonprofit then I will consider it a success. But I won't stop there; I am confident that if you read this book and apply the methods within, you will raise much more than 'just a little bit,' and on a much more consistent basis. Regardless, many of the tips, tricks, and ideas within will be applicable to your nonprofit with minimal effort and amazing results. But don't trust me, you'll need to see for yourself.

My name is James and I've served as a Director of an award-winning charity for several years. When I first joined the charity we were a small, modest charity whose impact was limited to the local government housing estate that our office resided within. Fast-forward a few years and we have more than doubled our income and, more importantly, our impact on our local community. This didn't come without struggle and a lot of learning, but with the recognition of a lot of large governmental and philanthropic organizations, the sleepless nights are fewer and further between.

With my experience in this charity's finances over the past few years, I can say with absolute confidence that it's entirely possible to build a sustainable, thriving nonprofit with the right fundraising strategies.

My background lies in finance. Although finance and nonprofits have traditionally been on opposite ends of the business spectrum, what I've learned is that nonprofits tend to suffer from a lack of research and investment that for-profit businesses would normally benefit from. The allure of large profits means that for-profit businesses suck up all the financial resources and investment, leaving nonprofit organizations perpetually underserved. Now, I'm dedicated to bridging this gap to help the charity sector expand and support nonprofit leaders in managing their organizations efficiently. My previous book, *Winning Grants: How to Write Winning Grant Proposals That Will Get You Funding for Your Nonprofit,* serves as a definitive manual for grant writing across sectors—and is a great companion to the one you're reading right now.

This is your shortcut to a sustainable fundraising blueprint. I'll break down 7 core fundraising strategies, diving deep into the most effective way to organize, plan, and execute each method. Each strategy is fully fleshed out, with detailed, practical action steps and insights to help you raise funds the right way for your nonprofit.

Success is not that far away, no matter what it might feel like right now. Follow the formulas outlined in the chapters ahead and the results will speak for themselves.

You'll quickly become well versed in fundraising techniques and be able to see which ones map best to your organization as I did for mine. Your team will learn invaluable lessons from the first rollout and, subsequently, develop the capability to deploy the strategies again and again so that you can create income streams you can count on. You'll be able to deploy the strategies any time your nonprofit needs a cash infusion, knowing that they will deliver a return—rather than hoping and wishing. Rinse and repeat. These reliable sources of funding will become the lifeblood of your nonprofit, allowing you to grow and reach even more of those who most need your services. Imagine expanding your mission to match your highest goals instead of turning them away, downscaling projects to match available resources, or parking ideas indefinitely.

Like me, you care deeply about those you serve. You know that despite all the good work your nonprofit does, it's just a drop in the ocean compared to what's possible. And you know the key lies in unlocking more funding and creating more reliable income streams.

In picking up this book, you've already shown that you're with me and you're serious about doing this. It's easy to bemoan the limitations we have to work with; not as easy to shift gears and embrace new ways of thinking and operating. To get different results, we must do something different, and step out of our comfort zones.

The deeper in you get, the more value you'll uncover as we dive into each of the 7 strategies and what it takes to succeed with each. Any and all of these strategies will work. It's up to you to choose which ones will be most effective for your nonprofit and go all in on applying them.

You're going to learn the building blocks of effective campaigning and how to utilize them to your benefit. I'll explain exactly what goes into preparing for a fundraiser, and walk you through the execution phase, step-by-step. I'll also introduce you to the world of partnerships. This is an often overlooked channel, but there are so many opportunities in this space once you know what to look for in a mutually beneficial partnership. Collaboration is central to success in the nonprofit field, and that applies at the individual level as well as at the macro level.

Of course, donors are essential to any nonprofit, so we'll devote some time to understanding the role they play, and how you can make it impossible for them to say no. Naturally, one key way to connect with donors today is through social media. We'll go through the various online platforms available, their strengths and features, and how you can leverage the world of digital to your advantage.

Campaigns remain an important source of funding. Certain factors may not be immediately obvious when it comes to effectively collecting funds through campaigning. We'll cover how to use campaigns to their full potential, bringing in both likely partners and donors. Likewise, annual giving can form an important part of the overall funding puzzle. I'll help you tap into this market effectively and your organization can start generating steady income on a regular basis.

Events have always been a mainstay of the fundraising scene. They're highly engaging, although often labor-intensive. You'll find out how to maximize return on your events while minimizing effort through strategic planning and execution.

And although it's easy to overlook donor retention, maintaining a healthy relationship with major donors and partners is vital to reduce the amount of ongoing work you need to do to fundraise for your nonprofit. We'll cover some best practices in this area while making them as simple and easy as possible to shore up your retention and, ultimately, financial resilience.

Once you pick a path, keep the momentum going. Take action—do something. Most people stop at consuming.

It's one thing to absorb information, but what makes a difference is what you do with your new knowledge. Going one step further and implementing these methods are what will set you apart and ensure the success of your nonprofit.

We'll begin with a quick overview of the state of fundraising today. What exactly is fundraising and why does it matter? And once we establish the many benefits of fundraising, we'll explore some inspiring examples of innovative fundraising to get your own creative juices flowing.

If, like me, you are an active learner, then I highly recommend you download this book on Audible and listen to it in tandem. Your retention of the information contained within and your ability to recall it when you need it will be much higher and ultimately lead to you becoming a more successful fundraiser.

Let's get on with it and officially begin the next phase in your fundraising journey.

1

WHAT ACTUALLY IS FUNDRAISING AND WHY IS IT SO IMPORTANT?

Can you guess how many nonprofits never make it past the 10-year mark . . . 1%, 5%, or 15%? Data from the National Center on Charitable Statistics (Ebarb, 2019) suggests that around 30% of nonprofits fail after 10 years. Many flounder due to a lack of strategic planning. It's not uncommon for nonprofit leaders to have blind spots when it comes to external forces and factors that ultimately become their downfall. After all, when you're laser-focused on the immediate needs of those you serve, and the daily crises that tend to erupt out of nowhere and require your full attention to solve, there isn't much bandwidth left over to stay attuned to the broader picture. Often, we don't think of other nonprofits as being our competitors, even though, ultimately, they're also vying for the same attention and dollars. We may fall prey to mission creep; after all, there are so many needs out there and so many deserving recipients. Or we might struggle to adapt our programs to meet evolving needs and keep up with the changing landscape. Sometimes we simply miscalculate what it truly takes to execute our mission. Although 'business plan' isn't part of the nonprofit lexicon, the same principles apply to our sector. It probably won't surprise you to hear that fundraising strategy and sustainability are rated as the top challenges among nonprofits, according to the Ewing Marion Kauffman Foundation (2017).

Where sales are the lifeblood of a typical company, fundraising is the lifeblood of a nonprofit. Longevity requires a sustainable funding strategy. In this chapter, we'll explore the nature of fundraising, the fundamental principles at play, and how fundraising has helped countless people across the world. You'll come away with a fresh appreciation for the art of fundraising, and a few ideas from other innovative charitable fundraising techniques to set you up for what comes next.

A BRIEF OVERVIEW OF FUNDRAISING

Let's start with a quick definition of fundraising. Simply put, it's the process of collecting money from donors, which could be either individuals or organizations—foundations, corporations, and even governments. And why do nonprofits need to fundraise? It's in the name. Nonprofits don't generate a surplus to benefit shareholders. Any profit is funneled back into the organization. Without fundraising, they wouldn't be able to function. After all, those served by nonprofits are not in a position to pay for the essential services received. Keep in mind that the main purpose of any nonprofit is to provide a public benefit of some type. Yet, nonprofits need funds to cover everything from wages and salaries to operating expenses for their premises and programs.

Ultimately, the more money they raise, the more good they can do in their given field, whether that's supporting underprivileged populations, environmental causes, human or animal rights, disaster relief, rare diseases, or whatever their focus might be. So if there's one thing nonprofits have in common, it's that fundraising must be a top priority to ensure their long-term survival. While they can qualify for tax exemptions and may receive benefits like discounts on the goods and services required to run their operations, there is no getting around the fact that it takes cash to keep things running.

Those in the profession of raising funds are known as fundraisers. However, fundraising within a nonprofit also includes responsibilities such as managing relationships with donors, managing volunteers, managing event logistics, and more. Their remit is broad. Likewise, fundraising is about much more than simply soliciting donations from others. There's much more to it. Nonprofits benefit in a variety of ways that go beyond the financial aspect.

For starters, fundraising helps to build awareness of your nonprofit. As you expand your reach—connecting with more people—and as that emotional bond grows, you'll find they are more likely to support your mission. Not just that, they may give more frequently, in larger amounts, or engage on a deeper level, perhaps even volunteering time and other resources as well. Donor loyalty is a wonderful byproduct of increased interest in your nonprofit more generally.

You can see how fundraisers provide a wonderful way to reach out to potential supporters, grow your donor base, recruit volunteers, and raise your nonprofit's profile. Not only that; the advantages flow both ways.

BENEFITS OF FUNDRAISING

As we just established, increasing awareness of your charity and your cause is a major reason to fundraise. That increased brand recognition can also lead to more media coverage and opportunities, further extending your visibility. After all, in order for people to give, they first need to know about your nonprofit. If they aren't aware of your existence, there's no way for them to pledge support. Fundraising helps get your name in front of more fresh eyes, as well as reminding existing supporters about how they can continue to help. Taking a step back, fundraising serves to lift awareness around your purpose as well. The people, animals, or causes you serve can all benefit from more of the public knowing about their needs, too.

Speaking of the public, fundraising is one way you can recognize the contributions and efforts of supporters and say thank you. Their commitment to supporting a cause makes your nonprofit's work possible. Charitable donations can be tax-deductible. But the bigger payback for donors is mental and emotional. Studies show that giving makes us feel better (Suttie & Marsh, 2010). The feel-good factor that comes with helping others is based in science. Doing good in the world stimulates the release of chemicals like dopamine, serotonin, and oxytocin into our brains. Giving back and the subsequent sense of making a tangible difference is actually beneficial for donors. It's one of the most fulfilling things we can do as humans. For corporations, participating in charitable fundraisers is also a great way to generate goodwill for their brand. It can engender positive feelings internally with staff, as well as externally with customers and other stakeholders.

Fundraisers create a space to bring together different communities in the name of positive change. Fundraising events offer an opportunity for the public to meet with your staff and volunteers, get a better insight into what you do, and see firsthand what direct impact their contribution could have. They bring your staff and stakeholders together, creating a sense of shared momentum and community, and raising morale. Fundraising provides a chance to make useful connections and collaborate with other like-minded organizations. It also offers an opportunity to ensure alignment on priorities and values. Likewise, this gives individuals donating their time or money a chance to meet other like minds who share similar interests and beliefs. Many friendships have grown from simply connecting through an event like a walk-a-thon. In fact, fundraisers can be a great introduction to something you have always wanted to try—swimming? baking?—but never quite got around to.

Conversely, fundraising can be an overlooked avenue for professional development. Every event is a team-building exercise in its own right, requiring everyone to pitch in and often pick up some new skills along the way. Volunteering time can provide an opportunity to share knowledge and practice skills in everything from administration and project management to marketing, copywriting, social media, and event management. There is even the possibility of making new professional connections that could lead to more doors opening in the future. Any time you create an opportunity for people to come together, you create the conditions for exciting possibilities like these.

So, when we give people the chance to make a difference simply by giving money or time, there's in actual fact a two-way value exchange at play. Giving back makes us feel productive as well as more connected to those around us. These social ties feed into both improved mental and physical health. It's also worth noting here that when someone gives, they also spur a ripple effect throughout their community, inspiring others to act in similar ways (Suttie & Marsh, 2010). This ultimately creates a compounding of altruism—what you might call the butterfly or domino effect.

ESSENTIAL FUNDRAISING PRINCIPLES

Now that we've established the purpose and importance of fundraising for nonprofits, let's examine a few essential principles you need to know to successfully raise funds.

Always begin by developing a motive and statement. What do you hope to achieve? Why—how will this tie into your mission? How do you intend to achieve this result? How is your charity placed in terms of capacity and capability to carry out the plan? What type of budget do you have to work with, and who will pay for the costs? Start with the outcome in mind and methodically work your way through the next steps, one at a time.

Focus on building impactful relationships. Keep your audience at the forefront. Consider their motivations and how you can best meet their needs. Where do they spend their time? How do they like to engage? How much do they know about your charity? What would be meaningful to them? People give in order to see the impact of their contribution, not just because they see a cause that needs support. The more effort you put into understanding them upfront, the more likely you are to be rewarded as a result. Cultivate connections before asking for anything. Lead by informing and educating. Always be respectful of their decisions to give or not, and their preferences around privacy and receiving communications.

Maintain a high degree of transparency and accountability. It takes time to gain trust but very little time to lose it. And once eroded, that credibility is difficult to regain. Protect your public reputation by acting with integrity, following any legal or regulatory requirements, and prioritizing the interests of supporters where appropriate. Be honest, truthful, and upfront whenever you are representing your nonprofit, particularly regarding how funds are spent. Be clear and precise about your work, how donations are managed, and how costs and impact shake out. Where donors indicate how they would like their contributions used, follow those wishes, and engage with them about alternatives if this is not possible. Disclose any conflicts of interest and decline gifts that would not be in the interests of your organization, supporters, or beneficiaries.

Act responsibly. Balance and manage your responsibilities, understanding the wider charitable landscape we operate within. Hold yourselves and others to high ethical and operating standards, including suppliers and partners. For example, ensure fundraisers are fairly remunerated, declare any gratuities they are offered, and do not receive disproportionate personal gain. This is how we raise the bar on fundraising excellence while demonstrating respect for donors and maintaining accountability—building their confidence in us so we can continue to ask for their support in the future.

These are just a few high-level concepts to keep in mind as you get deeper into this book. You'll get a full playbook later on with much more detail on every single step of the fundraising process, from soup to nuts. In the meantime, let's take a quick detour into some inspirational examples of innovative fundraising.

POPULAR EXAMPLES OF FUNDRAISING INNOVATIVELY

There is no shortage of tried-and-true fundraising tactics out there to follow—membership drives, mail appeals, telethons, events, and the list goes on. These are popular, established methods for a reason. But every so often, new, novel campaigns launch that capture public interest and make a real splash.

Remember the Ice Bucket Challenge? Videos popped up all over the internet of people pouring buckets full of icy water over their heads. Why? It was all in the name of raising awareness and funds for amyotrophic lateral sclerosis, more commonly abbreviated as ALS—also known as Lou Gehrig's disease (named after the baseball player). The general notion was that participants nominated someone else to take part, and if they failed to do so, they could forfeit by making a charitable donation. The tagging or calling out of friends to douse themselves in turn, made the campaign feel highly personal. It also helped fuel the spread of the campaign. The nature of the campaign also made for some rather entertaining videos.

ALS activists Patrick Quinn and Pete Frates co-founded the challenge, which went viral over the summer of 2014 (Frates went on to write a book about the Ice Bucket Challenge and his own experience with ALS). According to the *New York Times*, more than 1.2 million videos were shared on Facebook over a six-week period, and the campaign was mentioned more than 2.2 million times on Twitter with hashtags such as #IceBucketChallenge, #ALSIceBucketChallenge, and #StrikeOutALS (Steel, 2014). Wikipedia pages on ALS also saw massive increases in traffic during this time. All in all, the ALS Ice Bucket Challenge raised $115 million in donations. Since 2014, the ALS Association has committed more than $131 million toward its mission, including over $118 million for worldwide research collaborations (ALS, 2021).

The pandemic called for many nonprofits to get creative with their usual fundraisers. The charity DigDeep had everything lined up and ready to go ahead of its fundraiser for World Water Day in 2020—on March 22, to be precise. Nobody could have predicted a global pandemic throwing a spanner in the works. But they were determined to see things through in service of their $90,000 fundraising goal to ensure all Americans have access to clean running water.

DipDeep and their agency partner CauseMic devised a way to refocus the campaign strategy. The communication centered around an urgent, timely message, tying into the importance of handwashing and hygiene during COVID-19. With sanitation in the spotlight like never before, it was a prime time to raise awareness that not everyone has access to clean water. The campaign strategy also doubled down on leveraging DigDeep's database. The multi-channel approach spanned email, social media, text messaging, donation platform Funraise, and direct mail, enabling personalized messaging through segmentation and optimization. The strategy paid off, ultimately bringing in close to $150,000 in donations—blowing well past the original goal.

Or take the CFTK dance marathon. In North Carolina, the UNC Children's Hospital is served by the Carolina For The Kids Foundation, providing financial, medical, and emotional support to patients and their families. CFTK's annual dance marathon has been going for over 20 years and has become an institution of its own. But just as in the previous example, COVID-19 forced the foundation to rethink things. Historically, the event has consisted of an epic no-sleeping, no-sitting 24-hour event on the campus of UNC-Chapel Hill. But given worries about physical proximity to others and the fact that the campus had to shut down, CFTK adopted a digital approach, turning the dance marathon into a virtual format instead. This also helped save on production costs.

Let's look at one last example. Wings for Life, a charity supporting research into spinal cord injuries, put a unique spin on the classic charity run. Rather than compelling participants to achieve a certain distance, they simply had to see how far they could get within 30 minutes. After the half-hour was up, a chaser car set off, and once it caught up to them, then their race was deemed complete. The Wings for Life World Run 2021 raised more than 4 million euros for its cause and attracted a lot of attention thanks to its unusual rules.

In today's digital age where content can spread around the world almost instantly, the power of a popular viral campaign can't be underestimated. People crave novelty, and nonprofits that successfully harness the element of surprise and delight can go far with their fundraising efforts.

Summary

Nonprofits, rather than selling goods or services as a business, would provide public benefits and rely on donations to do so. These contributions can come from individuals or organizations, who in turn benefit from the strong sense of satisfaction and fulfillment that comes with giving back.

Fundraising is central to the success of any nonprofit. Not only does it help your organization meet its funding needs so you can deliver your services and programs, but fundraising also serves other equally important needs, like creating buzz and awareness and cultivating community goodwill—all of which in turn feed into a flywheel for sustainable success.

Next, let's turn to the tools you'll need to kick off an effective fundraising program.

2

THE ESSENTIAL TOOLS OF A FUNDRAISER

> *"Alone we can do so little; together we can do so much."*
>
> — HELEN KELLER

Fundraising is a team sport. It's not an activity you undertake alone. You'll also need the right tools for the job. Just like a mechanic, doctor, chef, or builder relies on their go-to gear, you should develop your own set of tools and maintain them well. This chapter is devoted to exploring the tools of the trade, so you can start automating more tasks and processes, reach new audiences, and ultimately solicit more donations for your nonprofit.

BENEFITS OF FUNDRAISING TOOLS

Let's start with an obvious one. You can raise money through all sorts of platforms. Donations serve as the fuel for your mission, so the wider you can cast your net, the better. For example, online crowdfunding platforms like GoFundMe have a large user base already that you can tap into, who are already primed for charitable giving. We'll dive into specific platforms in a bit more detail later in this chapter. Greater visibility is another benefit. Marketing and promotion may not come naturally, but it's essential for any organization, especially those that ultimately rely on the goodwill of others. If people aren't aware of your nonprofit, or your name isn't top of mind for them, they're unlikely to give.

You can also nurture better connections with donors, which is essential for cultivating loyalty. These days, connections are frequently made and maintained online. People are more digitally active than ever. Here are two telling statistics. According to Pew Research, 85% of Americans go online on a daily basis—and 31% say they are "almost constantly" online (Perrin & Atske, 2021). Make sure you're meeting your donors where they are. That doesn't mean your nonprofit needs to be constantly posting content. You don't have to be on every social media platform. Simply be strategic about where, when, and how you show up in order to stay relevant to your audience, and when they engage, continue to engage with them to keep the conversation going.

Detailed reports on gifts, funds, and campaigns are one of the top benefits that fundraising tools can offer. All good tools will incorporate in-depth analysis capability to help you analyze your results and refine your approach. You should expect to be able to tweak or create your own custom reports based on your needs, serving up more detailed insights that help you spot trends, and make better decisions to optimize future campaigns.

Finally, the right tools can enable faster communication and more cost-effective planning. We've highlighted the role technology can play in communicating more closely with donors and prospects. It can also help when it comes to communicating with staff and stakeholders. Internal communication can become fragmented, especially as your nonprofit grows, so don't overlook this area when considering what tools you might want to leverage. And of course, planning and managing projects and campaigns can always benefit from having a solid, central point where all key action steps and resources are housed. General communication and project management tools will typically get the job done here; the same principles apply to both private and public sector needs.

THE TOOLS OF A SUCCESSFUL FUNDRAISER

Many nonprofits cobble together various general business software programs to run their operations but quickly run into limitations when it comes to the fundraising side of things. Keeping track of donations and mailing lists can get unwieldy fast. That's where specialist software comes in. Fundraising software comes in many guises and there are plenty of tools out there targeted at nonprofits. Some are complex and include a wide array of features, while others are more single-minded, specializing in one or just a few aspects of fundraising.

Investing in fundraising software will pay off. In a survey, 99 percent of nonprofit professionals said that having fundraising software in place positively impacted the total amount of donations they collected (Finch, 2015). Once you determine your needs, assess the available solutions, and decide on which options will help you accomplish your goals, you'll be able to start simplifying and streamlining your current processes. This doesn't just go for online fundraising. It can apply to in-person outreach and events as well. This will reduce the amount of work you need to put into your campaigns, double handling or busywork relating to backend processing and create more free time to focus on high-value tasks.

How, exactly, you might ask? Here are some of the main ways.

Software can make it easy to set up attractive campaign pages that showcase the need for donations. Donation forms usually provide a way to instantly give via credit card or other payment options. Usually, these collect donor contact details and allow them to select an amount and choose a one-off or recurring gift. Donation buttons serve as a call to action that link to your donation page and can be placed in strategic positions on various pages. If you're running some kind of event, then fundraising tools can help with building a landing page, enabling registrations, selling tickets if it's a paid event, communicating with attendees, and generating reports about the event.

Every donation should be swiftly acknowledged with a thank you of some kind. Everyone likes to have their generosity acknowledged, and these days, they expect it —quickly. Ideally, if someone donates on your website, they would receive a receipt by email almost instantly. It may take some time and effort to set up the right technology for this workflow initially, but once it's done, it will create a much better donor experience. You want to nurture a relationship with the aim of converting a one-off donor into a regular donor. This is an area to invest in.

Collecting donations is one key area. Another is managing donor information, and we'll explore CRM systems in more detail shortly. Fundraising tools can play a key role in helping you reach the right people at the right time with the right message. The more you automate the managing and tracking of your communications and campaigns, the more ROI you'll see. Without the right tools in place, your ability to scale will be limited. Put simply, you can reach more people and make a targeted ask with the help of software that helps you build and maintain lists of prospects. You should be able to narrow them down by frequency or recency of giving, zero in on anyone who gave last year but not this year, and so forth. You can then personalize your communications based on what you know about who you're targeting. Remember the Pareto principle; 80% of your donations typically come from 20% of your donor base. Filter your database, cultivate your best prospects, and focus your efforts.

Fundraising software can also help with processing donations. A gift could be automatically acknowledged with a receipt and then sent to your accounting software, saving you from doing these steps manually, and eliminating the risk of human error. Look for a program that can handle various types of donations, such as pledges, credits, in-kind donations, split gifts, restricted gifts, or matched gifts. Most general-purpose accounting software isn't built to handle these types of gifts. Consider how donors like to give, and how you can enable that. Let's say someone wants to sign up for a regular monthly pledge. In that case, you'll need a solution that can handle the recurring charge, ensuring it's processed each month, that the funds are then transferred to your account, and triggering a donor receipt.

Given that most people own and use mobile phones on a daily basis, consider setting up a text-to-give channel. Collecting donations via text message creates another simple avenue for fundraising, both for campaigns and ongoing efforts. Another digital tool to consider harnessing is crowdfunding. This is when you rally a large number of people to contribute to your cause, usually online. Crowdfunding can supplement your existing initiatives, or you might set up standalone crowdfunding campaigns. We'll cover the power of peer giving toward the end of this chapter.

Note that payment processor Stripe has special charity pricing for registered nonprofits, as well as advanced reporting tools. PayPal includes nonprofits in its Giving Fund, offering another way for people to discover your cause, and it integrates with many CRM solutions. Square's own CRM can sort donors by giving criteria, so you can contact segments based on their engagement with your organization.

Specialized software can help you analyze your tactics, breaking down campaigns and channels, yielding actionable insights to inform your next efforts. There are even prospect research tools that offer wealth screening—taking data from the public domain, analyzing trends, and pinpointing potential donors who could be good targets.

For nonprofits that rely on grants or are interested in building up this source of funding, there is dedicated grant management software to help you stay on top of applications. You can set up and assign tasks, reminders, and deadlines. If it's difficult keeping tabs on proposals and funding status—it's easy for these to fall through the cracks when you have many other things on your plate—let technology assist you so that you can submit more funding requests and increase your odds of success.

CRMS FOR DONOR MANAGEMENT

Customer relationship management (CRM) software can provide a single centralized hub with a unified view of all contacts—not just donors, but volunteers, beneficiaries, and other stakeholders. It can serve as a one-stop shop for follow-up tasks, too. Most are cloud-based, so anyone in your organization can access the information anytime, anywhere. Some CRMs do involve a bit of a learning curve, so factor this into your planning.

One of the top benefits a CRM offers is an easily accessible home for complete donor information. A CRM system can track basic information, like someone's name and contact details, as well as a full track record of their historic involvement with your nonprofit. Beyond just giving history, you should be able to see their relationships with each other. Your database, for example, might include various members of the same family, or multiple employees of the same company. If you knew Michael and Betty both work for Acme Corp, and that Michael's employer matches his donations, then it's safe to assume that the same would apply to Betty. This is a much more dynamic and user-friendly option compared to spreadsheets. Building sophisticated user profiles and tracking their interactions with your organization calls for a more robust tool. This way, you can build stronger relationships and communicate more effectively and efficiently.

Use your CRM to segment contacts and deploy targeted communications. Take into account communication preferences, giving preferences, event engagement, business affiliations, and other relevant factors when individualizing newsletters, appeals, and receipts.

Importantly, a CRM should be able to produce a range of high-level reports, as well as provide granular insights into individual profiles. These will help you better understand your supporter base and refine your fundraising plans. How often do donors give? How much do they give at a time? These are questions a CRM can help answer. And you'll be able to track the results of campaigns—which you can also share with donors to demonstrate the impact of their contributions.

PEER-TO-PEER FUNDRAISING PLATFORMS

Peer-to-peer (P2P) fundraising is a specific type of crowdfunding and a relatively new arrival on the scene. Today, anyone can set up a fundraising page online and solicit donations for a cause. That means individuals can create their own fundraisers on behalf of your nonprofit, tailoring their appeals based on their personal experiences. They then share these online, through email and social media, spreading the word and collecting donations. The funds raised may go toward a specific campaign, or to your overall organization. You'll often see these in action when someone is doing a charity race, for example, or even taking part in a campaign like Movember, when people grow mustaches in the month of November in support of men's health issues, such as prostate cancer or testicular cancer.

P2P can be a highly effective strategy for raising funds. One key advantage is the opportunity to acquire new donors. P2P fundraising creates an organic extension of your organizational fundraising efforts. Individuals share their fundraising page with their family members, friends, and other peers, which could ultimately net your nonprofit fresh donors who are new to the cause. Their networks start to become your networks, too. These types of fundraisers ultimately hinge on personal connections—the trust between the person raising funds and their peers who choose to donate. After all, aren't you more likely to give to a cause when you know someone close to you supports it?

It would be unrealistic to expect every single contact of yours to donate to your P2P fundraiser. That said, getting people to talk about a cause is a huge step in the right direction. Raising awareness, fostering dialogue, and encouraging sharing are all great wins. Make sure individuals have the information they need to talk accurately and powerfully about your mission, so they can help educate their networks. Many of those contacts are likely to want to learn more about your nonprofit (and may even go on to contribute after that). Optimize all your social media profiles to capitalize on the increased attention. Encourage people to like and follow, or sign up to your email list, so you can continue to communicate with them and stay in their orbit. Growing your social media presence is a worthy secondary goal for any P2P campaign.

To really capitalize on the increased brand exposure, ensure that key elements of individual P2P campaign pages retain your nonprofit's branding. Visual attributes will do most of the heavy lifting in terms of brand recognition, so pay attention to your logo, typeface, colors, and images. Keep these elements consistent across campaign pages, fundraising pages, donation checkout pages, and all other touch points. Between a strong brand identity and a known, trusted giving platform, people will be more likely to feel comfortable pulling out their credit cards.

When a P2P campaign ties in with an event, it can also help bump up attendance numbers as well as raise funds. If you use dedicated event software, see if it connects to your P2P fundraising platform, so you can share data and streamline workflows. For example, you could then invite your P2P donors to your event. The P2P funds could help pay for the event itself or be added to the total amount raised through the event.

Think of P2P supporters as ambassadors for your organization. Treat this as an opportunity to learn more about them. They will often include personal notes on their fundraising pages about why your cause means so much to them, which is a valuable insight into their motivations that you can record in your donor database. It's this level of personal connection that makes P2P fundraising so successful. They're willing to share their beliefs and values widely, putting a personal face (their own) to your cause. So, be sure to reach out and thank them for their efforts after their campaign ends. They've bought into your mission deeply enough to go out and solicit on your behalf, and that deserves acknowledgment.

P2P can be a low-cost way for your organization to expand its reach and build credibility with more potential supporters. Campaigns are run entirely online, requiring little from your staff, so they can continue working on other initiatives during this time.

It offers a way for individuals to support a nonprofit without necessarily giving their own money, instead leveraging the trust they have with their networks. The proof is in the numbers. For instance, the average fundraiser on the DonorPerfect platform raises $568 (Orlando, 2021). And there are many other platforms you can use:

- **Qgiv** is a comprehensive fundraising platform catering to online and P2P fundraising as well as events, including auctions and mobile bidding. Set up branded event pages, email campaigns, leaderboards, live fundraising thermometers, milestone badges, and more. It can integrate with your CRM, email marketing platform, QuickBooks, and other programs—to name a few.

- **Salsa** provides a host of features for fundraising, advocacy, donor and event management, and marketing automation. It closely integrates with Salesforce. P2P features include individual and team donation pages, event registration pages, coaching messaging, content syndication to related organizations, and widgets to enable corporate employee donation matching.

- **Springly** is an all-in-one nonprofit management software focused on membership experience. That includes CRM, event management, fundraising and membership capability, and communication tools.

- **Fundly** is designed for online campaigns, with fundraising pages heavily featuring photo and video galleries and slideshows—you can add content straight from Facebook, YouTube, and Vimeo. Donation forms can be integrated directly into Facebook.

- **Grassroots Unwired** caters to mobile canvassing and constituent engagement, as well as fundraising, event management, and donations. Its 4EventDay app packs in a host of features like participant check-in, real-time connection with your CRM, offline capability, and simple sales and donations.

- **OneCause** offers a range of features and reporting for events, from planning and promotion through to ticketing, tables, registration, and checkout. Online fundraising is covered, too, with their virtual fundraising features, as well as text-to-give, silent auctions, and mobile bidding.

- **Donately**'s fundraising solution, as the name might suggest, prioritizes the donor experience. Along with fundraising pages, you can build multistep forms, embed them on popular website platforms like WordPress and Squarespace, and accept payments through a range of providers including Apple Pay and PayPal. Donately also integrates with tools like HubSpot and Google Analytics.

- **Classy** allows for flexible fundraising pages with photo, video, and blog updates, along with inbuilt social sharing, live leaderboards, and progress charts. The platform provides encouraging tips and coaching for fundraisers, and you can set up your own tailored versions through email for them.

- **GoFundMe** is perhaps the best-known and most popular P2P platform, often used to raise funds for personal emergencies as well as charitable organizations. It is free to use, with a transaction fee automatically deducted from each donation. GoFundMe offers access to a global community of more than 100 million people. Charities can also access donor and fundraiser reports.

- **Bonfire**'s unique fundraising platform lets supporters create and share T-shirt fundraisers on your behalf, using the Bonfire graphic library and product catalog, with all the money going to your nonprofit. You can highlight individual campaigns on your organizational profile, be notified about every new campaign, and see details about each supporter.

- **Funds2Orgs** is another niche platform for shoe drive fundraisers—collecting new or lightly worn shoes. These are then picked up and sent overseas to developing countries, primarily to women-owned micro-enterprises. Funds2Orgs provides a welcome kit and weekly tips, plug-and-play social media posts, templates, and a dedicated fundraising coaching team.

Summary

While fundraising is ultimately about connecting with other people, technology can do a lot of the heavy lifting for you. Make sure you stay up to date with the latest tools available and how they can help your nonprofit save time and money. You'll be able to fundraise much more efficiently when you leverage these to their full capacity. There are many excellent general fundraising software programs on the market, as well as specialist CRMs to assist with donor management, and an ever-growing list of peer-to-peer fundraising platforms to take advantage of.

When scoping out potential tools to integrate into your operations, consider the size of your organization and the skill set of your existing staff. Smaller nonprofits may not need all the bells and whistles of a more comprehensive program, for example. Look for free trials so you can test run tools, checking how user-friendly they are and how well their features mesh with your needs. Some may only support online activity, for instance, while others cater to a wider range of use cases. Take the time upfront to determine what are must-haves for your nonprofit, which are nice-to-haves, and don't get dazzled by flashy features that don't tick these boxes. Consider your existing tools and whether they can integrate to create a more seamless experience for you and your staff.

Now, you're ready to move on to the next phase: planning. It's time to shift gears and drill into how successful fundraisers are actually executed.

3

THE PLANNING STAGE

As the saying goes—failing to plan is essentially planning to fail. You need to know what you're aiming for if you want to get somewhere. Once you digest this chapter, you will be equipped to avoid this surprisingly common downfall. Particularly when you're working with limited resources, it's essential to make the most of them. The good news is, working within constraints can often breed creative solutions.

Good strategic planning will help your organization achieve its goals. These should flow out of your nonprofit's overall mission—your driving force. If your mission is to support new immigrants in education, a goal might be to offer scholarships for them, and an objective could be to award 10 scholarships over the next year. See how that provides a clear direction? Then, you can evaluate your assets and pinpoint any challenges. A SWOT analysis, for example, will highlight strengths, weaknesses, opportunities, and threats. Armed with all this information, you'll be well placed to create a strategic plan and a work plan to use moving forward.

When it comes to fundraising, planning well ahead will be the key to success. Consider this. When you're planning a fundraiser, what you're essentially doing is setting up and operating a small business venture. A temporary one, with a short shelf life—in fact, you know the exact date that it will be wound up—but an unarguably commercial one, nonetheless. Given that you only have a short time to drum up support, putting in the time upfront to plan things out could be the make-or-break factor. Organizing things as you go, especially when dealing with a large-scale project, is a recipe for stress. The more you can plan beforehand, in as much detail as possible, the more your future self will thank you. Get a head start, especially on the most time-consuming tasks, and make things easier for your whole team down the track.

So, what is the best way to approach planning your next fundraiser?

SET YOUR TARGETS

Start by defining your priorities. No doubt your nonprofit has a multitude of needs but narrow it down to one specific need that you'll raise funds for. Maybe, as in the early example, it's to fund scholarships for new immigrants.

Define a concrete financial goal for your fundraiser. How will you measure success? Look to achieve a balance between setting your sights high versus choosing a comfortable number that you know you can easily surpass. You might set a reasonable topline target which seems within the reach of possibility, as well as a stretch goal that reflects bigger hopes. Think ambitious yet achievable. Consider what other goals you may hope to tick off through this fundraiser as well, such as increasing donor acquisition and donor retention. There may also be other areas you would like to tackle, such as growing community engagement or building closer ties with staff and volunteers, which don't necessarily map to clear metrics.

SELECT A STRATEGY

Once you establish the amount you want to raise, it's time to think about how you'll achieve this. Where might this money come from? Brainstorm likely sources. How much might come from businesses, and which ones? What about grants? Who can you lean on within and beyond your community? What tactics will you employ to hit your funding goal this year? What about next year or the year after that? Can you roll out the same blueprint again, tweaking based on learnings from each iteration?

Choose what type of fundraiser to execute. (Over the next few chapters, we'll break down 7 specific strategies in detail.) Consider the mission of your organization, the talent and skills at your disposal, and your key audiences. These should all align; the intersection of these three elements will help determine what type of fundraiser you should select for the best chance of success. This decision could be made with broad consultation, or at the management level. Either way, give the matter the time it deserves.

Have you run a similar fundraiser before? Have your competitors? How was the public response? Will staff or volunteers require training? Do you have the tools and technology you need to pull this off? Will you need to solicit volunteers? Will you have enough funds to cover the costs? Are your best donors more likely to attend a gala or auction, a family-friendly fair, or a walk-a-thon? Are they time-poor and more inclined to simply write a check or donate online? Asking questions like these will help you zero in on the right type of fundraising strategy.

Whether you are focusing on individual giving, group giving, or corporate giving, among the most common techniques are online campaigns, direct mail, and tele-marketing. Many nonprofits hold one or two special events a year, which presents an opportunity to mobilize supporters who otherwise wouldn't engage, whether in person, virtually, or through a hybrid approach. Events can run the gamut from small to large and can include participatory events (such as walks, races, or cook-offs). And of course, grant funding is another avenue you can pursue, although the timelines and outcomes here will be beyond your control. Avoid relying heavily on only one type of fundraising, especially if that source could suddenly dry up, putting your nonprofit's financial health in jeopardy. But conversely, spreading your efforts too thin—going too wide with a scattergun approach—is unlikely to result in success.

Identify the key message for your fundraiser, which again will be informed by your mission and goal. Don't get bogged down by the details. Instead, focus on the why—ending discrimination or hunger, protecting animals, providing employment, etc. Highlight the donor's role in all this; their contributions enable the work—they are the real heroes. Reinforcing this consistently will help make it clear why people should support your cause, inspire them to act, and help them to spread the word, too. A rousing message is ultimately what will spur people to give.

Note for US nonprofits: You may need to register in any relevant states before going any further. Most states today require nonprofits to do so before asking for donations from their residents.

BUILD A PLAN

Now, it's time to translate the strategy into a concrete plan—a campaign calendar. A solid plan gives you a reference to work from, serving as the sole source of truth for everyone involved in making this fundraiser happen. When you're in the midst of juggling all the logistics, this will be a sanity saver. The combination of documented tasks and timelines will help when motivation starts to flag, or the team starts to lose focus.

Set a start and end date for your project, factoring in sufficient preparation time as well as some time afterward for reflection and analysis. In the preliminary stages of planning, you might specify milestones like "mid-October," and adjust these to specific dates closer to the time as the plan takes shape. Your plan should include labor time, as this will require a significant commitment from your staff and potentially volunteers. Be as thorough as you can. Note down anything that needs to be accounted for, no matter how minor. It's a clever idea to schedule any labor-intensive events or initiatives early in the campaign when energy levels tend to be at their highest.

When planning how to promote your fundraiser and get traction, choose your channels strategically. How can you reach those who are most likely to give, purchase, register, attend, and spread the word? There are traditional media like TV, radio, and print, as well as posters and flyers, and of course direct mail and phone. Online, there are plenty of options, from email and social media to paid digital advertising and partnering with influencers. Plan to start promoting a few weeks before your fundraiser officially begins, to build interest and get word of mouth flowing.

Then you can dig into brainstorming any hurdles that may get in the way and slow you down. Do you anticipate running into certain challenges based on previous experience? Is gaining media attention often a struggle? What about connecting with specific target audiences, like Generation Z? Or donor retention? Once you establish the main concerns, how could you go about proactively addressing these?

CREATE A BUDGET

You know what type of fundraiser you want to deliver, and how much you want to raise through it. Now, it's time to consider how much it will cost your organization to execute. The larger the initiative, the more resources it is likely to consume. But even the leanest campaigns still require an investment of time and money. Getting these projections right will be critical if you hope to hit your fundraising goal. Any blowouts will impact your profit.

If you've previously planned and delivered similar fundraisers, retrieve data from those. Look at the budget and the performance of the iterations that came before to anchor your next one—revenue, expenses, profit, and how these compared to the original goal.

Once you have come up with estimates for all expenses, work out the projected net revenue. Refer back to the goal—your original target for this fundraiser. If there is a gap between these numbers, then it's time to get to work to make up the shortfall. This could mean cutting back on certain costs or aiming to raise more. Calculate how your team could balance project spending to maximize the end profit.

As you refine your budget and work plan, bringing the details into sharper focus, adjust your plans accordingly. It's especially important to account for any additional costs that arise. Adding branded merchandise to the strategy? Incorporate line items for designing, manufacturing, and shipping.

For major campaigns, break down your revenue goals by phase. For example, the majority of funds may be raised through major gifts early on.

ASSEMBLE A TEAM

Bring together a project team who will execute the fundraiser together. They don't need to be experts in fundraising, but they should bring to the table skills that will help propel the campaign forward. For example, some key skills that will prove valuable include marketing, communications, writing, public relations, social media, design, photography, and videography. An external expert can be a useful addition to the project team as well. For example, you might bring in a consultant to assist with planning, researching key donors, or helping with turning the plan into concrete actions. Be transparent about why everyone is there, so they can make the best contribution. As you recruit more people, you can use their commitment to rally others to join the team, too. Highlight the impact you plan to make with your fundraiser and the anticipated benefits. Be clear about what you're asking of them. Set expectations upfront and respect their time and energy.

Effective delegation will be essential to success. Break down the various workstreams and assign specific to-dos to your staff. Defining clear roles and responsibilities for each team member will empower them to take decisive action and keep things moving forward. Certain areas can be designated the domain of an individual or a small group–depending on their interests and strengths. Create key performance indicators (KPIs) for people where it makes sense. For example, a team member might aim to pitch to a certain number of prospects by a certain date. These KPIs can be mapped out and aligned with the overall project timeline.

EXECUTE

Once everyone is clear on what they need to do, and when, the wheels are really in motion—procuring the materials and locations for events, creating collateral, setting up donation pages and forms, and so forth. Project leaders should check in regularly with team members. Of course, conducting group meetings is a must, but individual check-ins are important, too. This can help with identifying any issues early on, taking preventive or corrective action, and ensuring things progress according to the timeline.

Once launch day rolls around, you'll start to see all your hard work pay off. This stage is usually incredibly gratifying after the weeks or months of toiling behind the scenes. So, be sure to track and celebrate progress during this phase. Individuals can keep a running tally of how many prospects they've contacted or how much money they've raised to date.

FOLLOW UP

Your plan should also account for closing things off post-fundraiser. After your campaign wraps up, it's not over just yet. This is the point when you review the total amount raised and share the results. Hold a debrief session to go over what went well, and what could have been improved, but keep the focus positive and congratulatory. Reward the team for all their hard work. Think about how best to show your appreciation, depending on how individuals prefer to be recognized. In some cases, coming together to celebrate as a group may be appropriate. And of course, thank anyone else who contributed to the fundraiser's success, like partners, suppliers, board members, and major donors.

Summary

Pulling off a successful fundraiser takes work and a lot of planning. If you want to reach and exceed your goals, you'll need to set clear objectives, be realistic about the resources at hand, and devise a detailed plan, complete with granular tasks and deadlines that ladder up to the official public launch of your campaign. And of course, you will need to assemble a team of enthusiastic experts to help deliver it. After the fundraiser ends, be sure to document any lessons learned, so you can refine and improve when it's time to do it all again.

Next, we will start to investigate specific strategies for raising funds. I've selected the best, most efficient strategies to highlight over the coming chapters. As we touched on briefly, there are many tried-and-tested methods to solicit donations. You may even have tried some of these proven strategies before, or simply be curious about others. If an established strategy didn't yield the results you hoped for, don't write it off just yet. Keep reading to find out the exact formula behind it. Odds are, there was a step you weren't aware of, or didn't fully execute. Once you get that missing piece into place, it will make all the difference.

4

STRATEGY #1: THE PARTNERSHIP

"We make a living by what we get, but we make a life by what we give."

— WINSTON CHURCHILL

While collaboration and partnership has long been recognized as catalysts for success, perhaps no words illustrate the power of collaboration and partnership better than the ancient proverb that says "If you want to go fast, go alone; if you want to go far, go together." As anyone who's taken on a complex endeavor knows, having the right partnership is essential to the outcome of the project.

It's likely you already know what I'm talking about. If you've been lucky, you might have experienced the incredible power that results from working with the right person or organization. But there is also a chance you've drowned in work you could have avoided had you collaborated with others or have felt the deep frustration of dealing with the wrong type of people for your project.

Regardless of your past experiences, this chapter will guide you on how to unlock the true potential of partnerships. As with all strategies in this book, remember that no one size fits all. Your organization may team up with one key partner or cultivate a network of aligned partnerships to address different needs. Some partnerships might run for a set amount of time, while others may be open-ended.

In this chapter, you'll discover various types of partnerships and learn how to find the perfect fit for you and your organization. You'll also gain insights into building mutually beneficial and enduring partnerships, as well as crafting persuasive partnership pitches for the best odds of success.

THE BENEFITS OF PARTNERSHIPS AND COLLABORATIONS FOR NONPROFITS

Partnership and collaboration can help your nonprofit advance its mission, providing both financial and nonfinancial stability and expanding what you previously saw as possible and attainable.

Though each nonprofit will have its own set of reasons for collaborating with other organizations and individuals, some shared benefits will apply to most.

- **Visibility through cross-promotion:**

By collaborating, you gain access to your partner's network and vice versa. Being featured on their website, social media channels, intranet, and newsletters means you will gain exposure to a fresh audience, generating new interest in your activities and programs.

- **Enhanced goodwill:**

Whatever trust your partner already holds in the eyes of its internal and external audiences, your nonprofit will benefit from it as well. The announcement of a partnership can even serve as an appealing hook for media outlets.

- **Credibility boost:**

Partnering with a well-established brand can significantly boost your organization's credibility. Newer and smaller nonprofits will want to leverage this partnership to build a reputation faster than they would on their own, as it lends credence to their efforts.

- **Strength in numbers:**

Smaller nonprofits often struggle to be heard and make an impact. However, odds are other charities out there are working in the same or adjacent specialties as yours. By banding together with like-minded organizations, you create an opportunity to amplify your collective message. The more organizations you unite with, the louder your advocacy voices will ring, ultimately increasing your impact in the community.

- **Mutual accountability:**

Running a nonprofit can be hard. However, when everyone buys in and gets involved, there is more accountability to drive lasting change.

- **Fresh ideas:**

Inviting new people with diverse experiences, perspectives, and backgrounds to the table infuses your organization with fresh fundraising concepts, opening the door to novel ideas and solutions.

- **Unexpected synergies:**

The possibilities here are endless. You might discover a prime referral opportunity—i.e., your nonprofit serves the unhoused, while your partner offers a job training program. You could direct constituents to them for additional support and vice versa or combine existing programs for increased effectiveness.

- **Cost saving:**

Partnering allows you to save on administrative and operational costs. You can share supplies and workspace, or access better pricing for products and services by pooling resources with your partner.

- **Grant funding:**

Building relationships with like-minded nonprofits can make your application stand out amidst fierce competition. In a study of grant-making foundations, 69 percent actively encouraged collaboration among grantees and 42 percent of these said they sometimes required partnering as a condition for awarding funding (Ostrower, 2005). Moreover, not all sources of funding are open to all, and forging strategic connections opens doors to more opportunities.

EXPLORING DIFFERENT TYPES OF PARTNERSHIPS

Don't limit yourself when thinking of potential partnerships. Most of us will aim for the big brand names (and budgets) but these can be hard to access, and there could be greater benefits from joining forces with a small like-minded organization that shares common stakeholders.

Here are some ideas for you to explore:

1. Corporate partnerships:

Large companies often have generous budgets and may be able to contribute significant amounts to your cause. However, they also receive many requests for support, so standing out from the crowd, especially if your organization is lesser known or on the smaller side, may be a challenge.

2. Small businesses:

Local or regional businesses usually face fewer requests of this type, so competition is less intense. But the benefits of this type of partnership surpass the potential for easier access. Whether the business is a retailer, restaurant, or service provider, partnering with a small business in your area means that you will most likely share a similar niche, as you both have an interest in serving the same community or population.

3. Influencers:

Have you ever logged on to social media and been influenced to click on something or donate to a cause because someone you follow suggested it? If so, then you are already aware of the power of influencers. As with businesses, bigger is not always better. Micro-influencers, with followings from anything between 10k and 100k followers, might be easier to access and could resonate better with your niche.

4. Media organizations:

Local newspapers or TV stations can be invaluable allies. Provide them with compelling content that champions your cause so they can amplify your message to a wider audience.

5. Other organizations:

Government agencies, community organizations, or even associations and coalitions (such as those targeted at certain professions, or certain causes, like economic development) can also make good partners. Think broadly. For example, if your mission relates to improving literacy, a library could be a naturally aligned partner.

HOW CAN YOUR PARTNER SUPPORT YOUR NONPROFIT?

Say you've already scored a meeting with a potential partner for your organization. Right off the bat, they'll want to know what the partnership will entail and what you are asking of them. Don't arrive to the meeting waiting for their suggestions: show them a well-defined route and plan so they don't feel overwhelmed by additional work.

Consider the following ideas:

Direct donations are the most straightforward route. These could be cash, in-kind donations, or a combination of both. In-kind contributions can be physical items like food or equipment, or they can be intangible, such as with time and labor support. For example, you might receive pro bono advice on marketing or legal issues. You can also explore joint venture campaigns, where partners collaborate on fundraising initiatives. If partnering with a local coffee shop, for example, they set up a station to help collect donations for the fundraiser or round up their purchase to the next dollar.

Workplace giving is a growing channel that taps into a company's workforce. Companies can encourage staff to donate to charity and make it convenient by directly deducting a set amount from their paychecks. Large companies may even match employee donations, serving as a strong incentive for giving. Roughly $2–$3 billion is donated through matching gift programs every year, and a third of donors would give more if it would be matched (Double the Donation, 2022). Workplace giving can take place during a specific time-limited campaign or year-round. According to America's Charities, around $5 billion is raised through workplace giving annually. Establishing a payroll deduction with an established company can create a reliable income stream for a nonprofit.

Volunteering schemes can also give your nonprofit access to extra helping hands. You can use volunteers to help at events or help with behind-the-scenes operational work. There is, however, a caveat: When designing volunteering schemes, make sure you are not accidentally increasing your workload or assigning them tasks that will become frustrating. By aligning their skills with your needs, you increase the likelihood of future volunteering from them.

WHAT CAN YOUR NONPROFIT OFFER?

Remember, partnerships are mutually beneficial. So far we've talked about the ways your nonprofit can benefit from working with a different organization, but you should also have a clear idea of what you can offer to potential allies.

Partnering with a trusted nonprofit can improve how customers or clients view a company or organization. There's evidence to back this up: according to America's Charities, 90% of businesses indicate that partnering with reputable nonprofits enhances their brand. Through partnership, you can help them build a reputation within a community, influencing people to choose their products or services, thus driving sales or loyalty.

The benefit of cross-promotion also goes both ways. A corporate partner or sponsor can expect to receive prominent advertising opportunities in return for the partnership. Corporate partners or sponsors will often expect prominent advertising opportunities in return for their partnership. Display their name and logo on your campaign collateral, digital platforms, and other marketing materials to increase their visibility.

Charitable partnerships also tend to improve staff morale, leading to higher productivity and longer employee retention. Working for an employer that contributes to and cares about a good cause creates a source of pride and purpose among employees.

Keep in mind that corporate partners will often ask for data indicating the impact of their contribution. Document the benefits of the partnership both qualitatively and quantitatively. This can help foster long-lasting relationships.

Remember: Having a clear sense of what you can offer as part of a partnership is essential to getting the attention of potential partners and retaining them in productive, harmonious relationships.

10 STEPS TO SECURING QUALITY PARTNERSHIPS

Creating great partnerships for your nonprofit doesn't have to be complicated. Follow these steps to identify, approach, and secure partners, and ensure a healthy and beneficial ongoing relationship for both sides.

1. Start with a mission statement:

Your nonprofit should have a guiding mission statement that defines your goals. Whatever your North Star, use it when wading into partnership waters. Use it to identify potential partners who align with your purpose and can help you achieve your mission without distorting your message.

Example: If your nonprofit focuses on environmental conservation, look for partners that share a commitment to sustainability and ecological preservation.

2. Identify potential partners within your network:

Start by exploring close connections within your current network, including staff, advocates, and loyal donors. You can utilize their professional and personal connections to make introductions to key contacts.

Look for reputable companies with a community presence. Seek out companies that have a link to presence in your community. They could be exclusively local or be a larger organization with a branch in the area. Consider organizations that naturally align with your nonprofit's mission and could make ideal partners.

Example: An animal rescue organization could partner with a local pet store or a food bank with a nearby supermarket.

3. Find common ground:

The most successful partnerships share a purpose, audience, vision, or values. Identify where your views align with potential partners and brainstorm how a collaboration could deliver impact, benefits, or efficiencies.

Example: If your nonprofit focuses on youth empowerment, partner with an organization that shares a similar goal to provide mentorship or job opportunities for young people.

4. Ensure compatibility:

On that note, it's essential to emphasize the need for shared values. An oil company would not make a logical partner for an environmental nonprofit. Look for partners with aligned brands, missions, and cultures. No amount of money is worth a partnership that you wouldn't be proud to promote.

Example: An outdoor and sporting goods store would likely be a fantastic partner for an environmental nonprofit, as their customers likely have an interest in preserving the environment.

5. Present your vision and objectives compellingly:

Be clear about the needs of your nonprofit and express your aspirations for the future. Be clear about what it takes to run your projects and programs. If it requires a certain amount to ensure the viability of these each year, be upfront about that. Share key metrics, outcomes, and compelling narratives that illustrate the impact of your work, particularly if working with a previously existing partner. Humans are naturally driven by storytelling; make the most of that. You can then shift into articulating your request and what you have to offer in exchange.

Example: Share stories of individuals or communities who have benefited from your nonprofit and explain how additional resources could amplify your impact. You can even record testimonials of your beneficiaries so your partner or potential partner can put a face and voice to the data.

6. Show what you can bring to the table:

Highlight what your nonprofit can offer and how it can solve a problem or provide value to your potential partner. Clearly articulate the benefits and impact they can expect from the partnership. Look for the win-win. Even if it seems obvious, spell out exactly what's in it for the other party. This is especially relevant if they haven't engaged in similar partnerships in the past.

Engage in open discussions and listen to their goals. Get to know what impact or success would look like for them, how they prefer to engage with communities, and what aspects of your cause interest them.

Involve them in the development of the partnership engagement before actually moving into any solicitation. They may have useful ideas to contribute and getting early buy-in is the first step to a commitment. Leave space and time for discussion and further consideration: identifying a point person for communication will keep things moving along.

Example: If you run a food-focused nonprofit, highlight how you can make use of surplus food items from their business, reducing waste, and benefiting the local community.

7. Determine the details of the partnership and align expectations:

Agree on the level of donation, sponsorship, or volunteering that both parties find valuable. Clearly define each partner's role and responsibilities, as well as the intended outcomes of the partnership.

Example: Create a memorandum of understanding or contract that outlines the contributions and expectations of each partner.

8. Set up strategy meetings and execute the plan:

Collaborate on fundraising initiatives or events that benefit both parties. Get specific about deliverables, such as promotional opportunities and social media mentions.

Example: Don't leave things up in the air or assume you are on the same page without addressing it first. Where will you display their name and logo, and vice versa? Will you put out a press release? Who will distribute it? How often or how many times will you mention your partner on social media or in newsletters? What would success look like?

9. Get the campaign rolling:

Once you've found a suitable partner, finalized the details, and are ready to launch your campaign or event, it's important to assign tasks to each person involved. This lets each individual focus on a specific effort and leverage their unique talents and skills.

Example: Partnerships can take diverse compositions, but everyone should have a crucial role to fill. This can range from finding prospective donors and nurturing relationships with them to soliciting donations, recognizing contributors, engaging in community advocacy, managing media engagement, and conducting marketing and promotion through various channels.

10. Keep collaboration harmonious and productive:

Maintaining clear, open communication is the cornerstone of a great partnership. Remember to regularly step back and assess how things are going. Seek feedback and suggestions from your partner. Track the progress of your shared initiatives and the return on investment.

Example: Ask yourself the following questions and return to them periodically:

1. Are we delivering the solution we originally envisioned?
2. What has been the impact of our work so far, and how has it been received?
3. How can we effectively measure and collect data to assess our progress?
4. In which areas can we make improvements?
5. What aspects of our partnership are performing well?
6. What larger macro trends are currently shaping the landscape, and how should we factor them into our plans?
7. Do all partners feel empowered to contribute their insights and fulfill their roles effectively?

Summary

Partnerships, whether with fellow nonprofits, corporations, small businesses, or influencers, play a crucial role in helping your nonprofit create a broader impact and expand its reach. Strong partnerships can emerge from unexpected sources, often within your existing network or community. The more you understand and learn about your closest connections, the better the odds of tapping into a great potential partner.

Get a sense for what sponsors look to gain from a nonprofit partnership. Partnering with a charity benefits their interests as well. This understanding will assist you in crafting a mutually beneficial proposal. Focus on long-term transformation rather than short-term transactions.

Once you've identified promising partnership opportunities, be sure to nurture a relationship. Great partnerships are built on shared interests and thrive on consistent and effective communication. Regularly evaluate the partnership to ensure it continues to deliver value to all parties involved.

Our next fundraising strategy focuses on leveraging donors. When you're ready, let's delve into understanding their desires and motivations, so you can establish stronger connections, foster mutually beneficial relationships, and explore various approaches to attract new supporters for your fundraiser.

5

STRATEGY #2: BRINGING IN DONORS

Ever wondered what really motivates your top donors? Take a moment to step into their shoes and see things from their perspective. Understanding the mindset of a donor is a skill that every nonprofit professional should master. Believe it or not, supporters contribute for a multitude of reasons that go way beyond just the tax perks. It could be a personal connection to your mission that ignites their passion, the thrill of being part of a movement greater than themselves, or the desire to make a positive impact with their hard-earned dollars. Plus, donating to charities simply feels good. It's been scientifically proven that acts of generosity release dopamine, so we literally get a happiness boost from helping others.

According to a survey by Network for Good (2018), the top motivator among donors was being mission-driven. They're drawn to your organization because of its mission, but they stay when you consistently demonstrate commitment, reliability, and transparency. Being true to your word and acting consistently is the way to earn their trust. On the flip side, a lack of accountability is the main reason donors pull back their support.

Ultimately, what matters to most donors is impact. They want to see tangible evidence that shows them how their money is being used to help others in the world. When they know their money has been put to good use, they feel a sense of empowerment and like they're part of something bigger than themselves.

This chapter will help you delve into the complex world of donors to understand their motivations and desires and gain insights into how to create long-lasting and beneficial relationships with them.

Some donors are natural do-gooders, driven by an inherent altruism. It's their way of making a moral difference. Others have a personal connection to a cause and can often turn out to be your most passionate and loyal advocates. And a different group might be mostly interested in the financial incentives for making charitable contributions. Most donors can access a tax deduction, depending on the status of the organization they're supporting. And, evidently, these groups are not mutually exclusive and can often overlap.

Whatever their motivations, understanding your donors and creating strong relationships with them can truly make magic happen. Let's get to it.

WHY ARE DONORS SO IMPORTANT?

Why are donors so crucial in the world of fundraising? If you are reading this book, chances are you might already know or at least have a sense of the answer to this question. Still, donors are so important it's worth digging into the details.

First and foremost, donors bring in the funds that keep your organization running. Without them, it's tough to keep the lights on. Among them, loyal donors are the real gems and the ones worth fighting for. Their regular donations provide a consistent and reliable source of income—no more anxiously waiting for the next influx of money. When you can predict a certain amount of income each month or quarter, you can plan more effectively and focus your time and energy on your operational activities.

But that's hardly it. Donors also play a vital role in boosting your message, generating greater awareness, and funding. Technology has made it possible to encourage donors to easily spread the word by sharing their support online, reaching even more people. And let's not forget the personal touch. Never underestimate the power of a simple request to tell friends and family about your fundraiser. Even if only a fraction of a donor's network—family, friends, neighbors, acquaintances, and colleagues—are introduced to your organization, your organization can reach far beyond its usual borders. Finally, donors can bring new ideas into your organization. Sometimes, it takes an external perspective to spot opportunities for innovation and improvement. Those fresh eyes and fresh perspectives might be just what your organization needs from time to time. Donor relationships can also open doors to other exciting opportunities, such as corporate sponsorships and major donors. Don't underestimate the power of individuals and the potential connections they may have or the combined efforts they can make. Who knows what they could offer to support your cause?

THE IMPORTANCE OF LOYAL DONORS

I want to take a moment to explain the importance of long-term, committed donors and why they are worth the investment over one-off donations.

Regular donors demonstrate a remarkable commitment by giving significantly more compared to their one-time counterparts—an astounding 440 percent more, to be exact. Although recurring donations might have a lower individual value than single contributions, the power of consistent support far outweighs this difference. In fact, studies have shown that the average lifetime financial return from a recurring donor is just over $795, while that of a one-time donor amounts to only $147 (Philanthropy News Digest, 2018).

Moreover, acquiring new donors can be extremely costly —there is recruiting, training, managing fundraisers, and extensive marketing efforts. These expenses often surpass the cost of retaining your current supporters. Existing donors will always give your nonprofit the most bang for the buck. Every time you start from scratch with a new donor, you have to educate them about your work and build trust from the ground up. While donor acquisition should always be a priority, don't forget your current supporter base. Remember, one size does not fit all—take into account each individual's giving history when cultivating and maintaining donor relationships.

Think about long-term donors as friendships. Like the best relationships, they take time and effort to cultivate, but also yield the most rewarding outcomes—ones that can last a lifetime.

THE 6 MAIN TYPES OF DONORS

Donors can come from anywhere and take all shapes and forms. They will all have different reasons for giving, as well as different ways to do so. For the purpose of this chapter, let's break them down into six main categories:

1. Individual Donors:

These are the most common donors and, collectively, will form the core of your supporter base. While gaining or losing one here or there won't make a noticeable difference, they can add up to account for a significant chunk of your nonprofit's income. Once you secure a new individual donor and they make a gift to your organization, celebrate them and be sure of keeping in touch. Follow up with a personal thank you and explain how their gift will be used, and share information on upcoming events, initiatives, or programs.

2. Major Donors:

Major donors aren't secured in one fell swoop; they are frequently the result of years of sustained effort. Cultivating major donors takes time and effort, but it's worth it because of the large sums they can provide. Depending on the size, major gifts can change the trajectory of your organization. If you have the staff, select someone to work with major donors, conduct research, build profiles, nurture the relationship, and steward communications over the long run.

Unlike organizational or corporate donors, major donors have the freedom to give without committee consultations or sign-offs. This makes them an ideal choice if your nonprofit has an urgent, specific need. If a project truly resonates with them, they might even fund the entire initiative. Treat major donors as VIPs and remember that each donor is a unique individual and more than just a wallet. Connect with them on a personal level above all else. Major donors don't need a hard sell but will want to be kept up to date. Like any other donor, seeing the impact of their gift is powerful.

3. Corporate donors:

As for-profit businesses, corporate donors will require an exchange of value to secure their support. Typically, they will expect to receive advertising and publicity for their brand in return for their contribution. This could be as simple as promotion through your nonprofit's own marketing channels, or at the other end of the scale, having naming rights to a building or facility. That being said, some CEOs or senior leaders may have personal passions for specific causes. Leverage that motivator.

Regardless, corporate social responsibility is now a top priority, and businesses are expected to contribute to the communities they operate in—so it's worth considering how corporate donors fit into your fundraising strategy.

4. Foundations:

These institutions are often the unsung heroes of philanthropy. Candid (2020) reveals that there are over 100,000 foundations in the US, with over $80 billion to give out. They usually award grants only in certain key focus areas: mostly health and education, as well as those affected by economic disadvantages, including children and youth. When dealing with foundations, remember that accountability is key. Grant recipients often have the responsibility to demonstrate measurable outcomes, ensuring that the foundation's investment yields tangible results. Although grants for capital or operating expenses are less common, the potential for financial support remains significant. Remember that foundations themselves operate as nonprofits. Community foundations generate funds directly from the public, while corporations may establish foundations as separate legal entities. Additionally, private foundations, like the Bill & Melinda Gates Foundation emerge from the passion of individuals or families, carrying out their own impactful programs. Be sure to align your organization's mission with the foundations you approach.

5. Organizations:

While organizations are a lesser-known source of funding, they certainly deserve a starring role in your donor strategy. Trade or professional associations, coalitions, sports clubs, and even churches can emerge as unexpected champions. Cast your net far and wide and don't overlook community organizations.

6. Volunteers and advocates:

These passionate individuals are a valuable category of donor in their own right and hold a special place in the donor realm. For some, giving time rather than money is the best way for them to contribute, though this may evolve—depending on their personal circumstances.

The young and spirited often have an abundance of spare time and passion and may one day become a financial donor as their situation changes. Older people on fixed incomes might not just have free time but may even leave a lasting legacy through a bequest. Some of your volunteers may be volunteering mainly in order to gain credits or fulfill some type of requirement for work or school. If this is the case, you can play up this angle in your content and marketing to attract more similar volunteers. Remember, recognition is key. Acknowledge their participation and commitment. When volunteers feel appreciated, they can become the driving force that keeps on giving and helps recruit others as well.

HOW TO BRING IN DONORS FOR A FUNDRAISER

You already know the different types of donors out there and why they are so important to your nonprofit. So you may now be wondering: How do I bring them in? Finding new donors and getting their attention (and money) can be a frustrating experience: competition is fierce among nonprofits and donors' capabilities might be limited.

But you don't need to lose sleep over this. Let's break down the best ways to do it.

Start by identifying your main objective and mapping out your fundraising strategy (refer to Chapter 3). Ensure your messaging is donor-centric, appealing to what they care about and emphasizing the impact and outcomes of their giving. Your appeal should speak to their hearts, not just their heads. Remember that stories resonate most with people, so incorporate personal anecdotes and humanize your mission. Along with numbers and graphs, be sure to put a human face to your work, personalizing and humanizing the work you do.

Once you've developed your appeal, it's time to promote it. Consider your audience's preferences and determine the most effective channels for reaching and engaging with them. Begin soliciting donors through your chosen mediums.

Get your website ready to attract donors. Choose powerful images that showcase the people benefiting from your work. Don't forget to share touching stories and videos that truly demonstrate your impact. When you talk to your readers, speak directly to them, like you're having a conversation. Remember, you are appealing to their hearts. You could invite them to "learn about Alex's incredible fight for life" or "discover how your support is making a real difference in regenerating rainforests." You could even add some features to display the support you are receiving, showing recent donations in a dynamic feed or a friendly alert that says something like, "Hey, guess what? Riley from California just donated $50, which means 5 children in Benin will get brand-new shoes!" See the pattern? Frame the donor as the hero of the story; honestly, it's their contributions that make all the difference.

Since we are talking about your website, make sure your donation buttons grab attention. Go for bold colors and compelling calls to action such as: "Feed a child today," "Save the endangered black rhino," or "Send essential supplies to people fleeing their homes." Don't be afraid to try something extra, like a pop-up box alongside your donation buttons. Yes, it can seem intrusive, but every person who visits your website with the intention of donating will be grateful. Test it and see how it works for you.

Simplify those donation forms. Stick to the essentials: name, contact info, and payment details. The smoother and quicker the process, the higher the chances people will complete them. Don't forget to test them on mobile devices, as many people will be accessing your forms on a phone or tablet. Make sure to include a link to your donation page in all your communications. It's all about making it as easy as possible for people to contribute.

Make sure your emails are action-packed. Include multiple opportunities to take action, like donation buttons and attention-grabbing links. Many of us are subscribed to too many newsletters, so make sure yours are entertaining. Segment your email list so you can tailor your messages: you wouldn't send the same email to a fresh-faced donor as you would to a long-time supporter. Set up an automated welcome email that introduces new subscribers to your nonprofit's story and mission. Show them the impact of your work right from the start.

Don't just depend on social media and don't expect donations to come rolling in as soon as you hit publish on a post. Social media is often more of an awareness tool than a conversion one. Think about the importance of one-on-one. Consider incorporating phone outreach into your donor campaign. Depending on your team's resources, you can make individual calls or even organize a phone-a-thon. Speaking directly to donors over the phone gives you a valuable opportunity to explain how their gift makes a difference. Develop a base script for callers to ensure consistency and success. And don't shrug the power of merchandise. From mugs to keychains or tea towels, they are a fun way to get your message or brand to cut through the noise and get new donors interested. Make sure to include social media handles somewhere in there to make it easier for them to get in touch.

Make the most of your existing supporter base. Reach out to your loyal advocates, including board members, volunteers, and donors, and ask them to help spread the word. They're invested in your success, and sharing your cause with others is an uncomplicated and effective way for them to support you. Additionally, reconnect with previous donors. Just because someone hasn't donated in a while doesn't mean they've lost interest. It's possible that your nonprofit simply slipped off their radar, and they may even appreciate hearing from you. Don't hesitate to reach out and acknowledge their past support. One-time or lapsed donors are still potential supporters. Personalize your message as much as possible, mentioning their previous contribution amount, date, and how it made an impact.

Take the time to research and connect with promising prospects. Begin by reviewing your internal database and identifying those who have shown a likelihood to donate based on specific factors. Look into annual reports and newsletters from similar organizations to discover their key donors. (More on handling major donors coming up soon.) Extend your reach even further through collaborations with aligned organizations. Their audiences may be like minds who become your supporters as well. Refer back to Chapter 4 on building strategic partnerships or sponsorships.

Search for major donors. They make significant contributions and play a vital role in sustaining your funding. Start by identifying your most generous existing donors if you don't have a major donor portfolio. Who has given the largest sums? Screen your database and learn from your top donors. Then, do some prospect research to find others who might be inclined to give in a comparable and equivalent way. Once you scout out and identify optimal prospective major donors, develop a personalized outreach strategy. Building a connection and understanding their priorities and motivators is crucial. While you know they have the capacity to give, persuading them to take that leap requires a compelling case. Major gifts aren't randomly given; they stem from a profound connection between an individual and a cause.

Summary

It might seem like common sense, but it's worth reiterating: donors are the lifeblood of your nonprofit. They are essential for your organization's survival and the impact you make in people's lives. Understanding your supporter base, which can include individuals, major donors, corporations, foundations, organizations, and volunteers, is key. By knowing their motivations, you can tailor your campaign messaging to truly cater to their needs, finding your way into their hearts and wallets.

Don't be afraid to make bold requests, asking for their support in amplifying your message and mission. With a solid foundation of credibility and trust, many supporters will gladly step up as ambassadors and advocates.

Before moving on, think about your existing and potential donors. How can you improve communication with them? Are you reaching all your potential supporters, or have you settled in a comfort zone? And how can you turn your current one-off donations into sustained ones? Ask yourself these questions and think of ways in which you can put everything you've learned through this chapter into action.

We will now dive into the world of social media. While it's a rapidly changing landscape, there are timeless fundraising principles that apply across different platforms. By executing effectively and leveraging each channel, you can navigate any algorithm updates and maximize your online presence.

6

STRATEGY #3: THE DIGITAL FUNDRAISER

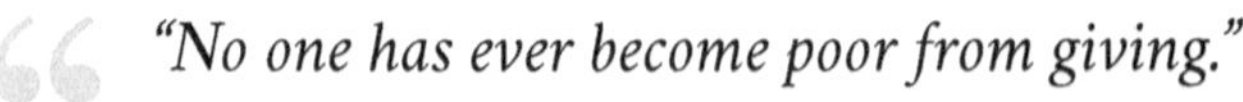

"No one has ever become poor from giving."

— MAYA ANGELOU

Social media has revolutionized countless industries, and the charitable sector is no exception. Gone are the days of relying solely on traditional media or partners to boost your publicity efforts. With social media, you now have the opportunity to have unprecedented control over your brand and messaging. Social platforms offer nonprofits a direct route to reach the public, allowing them to share their stories quickly, cost-effectively, and with great impact. They provide a unique opportunity to engage supporters, promote campaigns, and amplify your organization's message.

Consider this: a quarter of donors discover new nonprofits through mobile devices, while up to 55% of people who engage with a nonprofit on social media take meaningful action as a result (Nonprofit Source, 2022). The numbers don't lie: if you hope to organize a successful fundraiser and bring in new donors, then you can't overlook social media.

In this chapter, I will delve into the importance of social media in fundraising and explore how you can effectively harness different platforms for your charitable cause. When we refer to social media, we are talking about websites and applications that allow us to post, share, and engage with content. These platforms go beyond mere content consumption; they foster communication and community building. Among the most widely used social media networks, we have Facebook, YouTube, WhatsApp, Instagram, WeChat, and TikTok (Statista, 2022). In the ever-shifting landscape of technology, being on top of your social media game is nonnegotiable. While it can feel overwhelming, the guidelines and best practices I will provide in this chapter will help you navigate this essential arena.

THE ROLE OF SOCIAL MEDIA IN FUNDRAISING

Social media is an essential tool that has transformed the nonprofit sector, particularly in connecting with donors and supporters. These platforms enable individuals, organizations, and causes to amplify their messages and mobilize global support for fundraising. Through crowdfunding, peer-to-peer fundraising, and direct appeals, social media provides a dynamic platform for storytelling, community engagement, and donor participation. It has become an indispensable resource for making a meaningful impact in fundraising efforts.

Your organization is now able to reach more people than ever before. By mastering the art of creating engaging content, your brand can connect with users worldwide. Social networks thrive on content consumption and sharing, with individuals constantly reposting and sending links to their networks. Algorithms recognize engagement and amplify the reach of well-received content. By actively participating and being present, you increase your chances of being discovered. This, in turn, makes it easier to inspire your followers to take concrete actions, whether it's calling politicians, attending protests, or making personal changes. Even someone across the globe can contribute to your fundraiser with a simple click or sign a petition.

Unleash the power of storytelling to propel your brand awareness forward. By sharing the compelling narratives of your organization and its cause, you can ignite a sense of connection and empathy among your audience. Illuminate the personal stories of individuals whose lives have been positively transformed by your work and showcase the real impact you make. Through the art of storytelling, you have the ability to captivate hearts and inspire action. Share the driving force behind your nonprofit's inception, what motivates your current staff and volunteers, and how your fundraisers and programs have positively impacted the lives of those you serve. Show your donors that their support is valued and demonstrate the difference they make. Regular posts and updates will help you maintain a strong connection with them, fostering a sense of community even when you are countries apart.

Finally, these media platforms have made communication two-way. Rather than reading an advertisement in a magazine or staring at a TV screen, users can now voice their opinion and interest in various topics, allowing organizations to tap directly into their interests and concerns. This is known as social media monitoring or social listening, an approach that can help you refine your online communication. By paying attention to what individuals are already saying about relevant subjects, you gain valuable insights into how your nonprofit is perceived and what information your audience seeks. Monitoring direct mentions of your organization and campaigns is essential, but it is equally important to keep tabs on popular issues among your audience and the discussions among top influencers. With these insights, you can adjust fundraising messaging, target digital ads based on demographics or interests, and effectively engage your audience.

DIGITAL PLATFORMS FOR FUNDRAISING

While the social media landscape is ever-changing, it's worth knowing the most important platforms at the moment. Keep in mind, not every social media app might be the one for your nonprofit. Choosing the right one for you will depend on a number of different factors: whether your content is mostly text-based or visual; if you have a dedicated AV team; and the amount of content you can generate. Keep reading to learn more about the most important social media platforms right now and how to choose the right one for your organization.

Facebook's sheer size is obviously its biggest drawback, but the other benefits for nonprofits are the cherry on top. You can add a donation button to your charity's Facebook page, create custom stickers for Stories or even hold a real-time fundraising drive via Facebook Live.

Since it's owned by the same company that owns Instagram, both platforms can be integrated to facilitate your work. Keep in mind, however, that Facebook's user base is now slightly older. If your nonprofit appeals to younger audiences, it might be worthwhile considering some of the more visual platforms on this list.

Twitter is a fast-moving social media network that's particularly useful for breaking news and jumping on the day's trending topics. It is often favored by influential users in media, technology, and politics, so it can be an incredibly useful platform to connect with relevant figures in various fields. Use Twitter to advocate for your cause, engage in current events, and connect with other experts of organizations in the same niche. Twitter might be a great platform for your nonprofit if you are vocal and engage in current debates.

Instagram is particularly useful for nonprofits with visually compelling content. Nonprofits capable of generating impactful and captivating images and videos will thrive here. Organizations can leverage features like Instagram Stories, IGTV, and Reels to showcase behind-the-scenes footage, highlight success stories, and provide valuable educational content. The platform also offers the chance to add a donation button and to drive direct support from followers. As I mentioned, Instagram and Facebook can be integrated quite seamlessly.

TikTok is a fairly new addition to the social media scene but has soared in popularity quickly. Its TikTok for Good program offers account management help to nonprofits, along with advanced analytics and promoted hashtags. TikTok's user base is quite young so it might not be the best platform if you are looking to find new donors, though it could be quite useful for recruiting volunteers. Keep in mind that TikTok is all about short videos and live streams, so you will need to tailor your message to this format.

YouTube is just as much a search-based platform as it is a social media platform. This platform is great for sharing longer videos, tutorials, or how-to videos, and live streams. This content can include testimonials, success stories, behind-the-scenes footage, and educational videos. By consistently uploading high-quality videos, optimizing them with relevant keywords and tags, and sharing them across social media channels, your organization can create a thriving and engaged community.

Reddit is an extremely popular forum with a substantial user base that skews toward mostly a young and predominantly male audience. While overt self-promotion is generally discouraged, nonprofits can establish meaningful connections through authentic engagement and by hosting Ask Me Anything (AMA) sessions. These interactive sessions provide an opportunity for organizations to answer questions, share insights, and build rapport with their community. Be aware, however, that most Reddit users are anonymous, which can generate trolling.

Pinterest serves as a visually appealing platform that serves as a digital scrapbook and has a predominantly young to middle-aged female user base. It allows users to save content from your website and is particularly suitable for organizations operating in the arts or nature/conservation sectors, as it offers an ideal medium to showcase captivating photos, engaging videos, and informative infographics. You can also use Pinterest to promote merchandise and product sales as part of your fundraising efforts, especially if you can position them as gift ideas for key occasions like holidays or other seasonal events.

SOCIAL MEDIA ADVERTISING

Now that you know the main social media platforms for nonprofits, let's dive into the game-changing world of social media advertising. With a flood of content being created every minute, it's becoming increasingly challenging to stand out from the crowd. This is where paid promotion comes in. Each social network offers ways for brands to boost their content and reach a wider audience. You can target specific audiences and optimize your campaigns for different outcomes, whether it's reaching as many people as possible or maximizing donations. Start small, test, learn, and then scale up your efforts. Remember that algorithms are constantly changing, so mastering the art of social media advertising requires constant tinkering.

Make sure your website is ready to track the traffic and actions generated by your campaigns. Tools like Google Analytics are easy to use and can provide extremely valuable information. Don't overlook micro conversions like video views or visits to your donation form—they can be valuable interactions. And of course, don't forget about macro conversions like donations, newsletter registrations, and event signups. This will all provide valuable information on how to spend your money on advertising.

Think beyond social media and consider advertising through Google as well. Google Grants funding offers nonprofits $10,000 in free ad spending every month. With the average cost per click for advocacy ads being around $1.50, this could drive a significant amount of traffic to your website, potentially resulting in valuable donations. The process to qualify for Google Grants is not automatic, however, so you will need to apply and meet criteria, which exclude certain nonprofits like schools and educational institutions, government organizations, and healthcare organizations.

DIGITAL FUNDRAISING

Social media and other digital tools are not just great for communication and fostering community, but for fundraising, streamlining the donation process. and allowing you to reach potential donors like never before.

Your nonprofit's website is a crucial player in your digital fundraising efforts, so it's essential to optimize it for donation collection. Add strategically placed calls-to-action and donation buttons in prominent spots throughout your site and streamline your campaign landing pages and donation forms to make the giving process as simple as possible. Consider implementing payment pop-up boxes to enhance giving, and experiment with different visuals and copy to analyze which combinations yield the best results. Don't forget to thoroughly test your website on mobile devices as well as desktops: half of your traffic will come from mobile devices (Double the Donation, 2022). So if your website and its donation buttons perform poorly on mobile, you're missing out on valuable interactions.

Email marketing will be another key pillar in your digital fundraising strategy. Leverage your email list as a valuable asset. A good email marketing platform, even if not specifically designed for nonprofits, allows you to segment your audience based on tags like location, income, interests, and giving level, enabling customized communications. It should also offer scheduling features. Check at what time your email list is most likely to click on links or open the email to optimize your mailing times.

When crafting fundraising emails, put effort into creating compelling subject lines that are both descriptive/evocative and action-oriented. Emojis can boost open rates, and personalizing emails with recipients' names adds a personal touch. Remember that emails often display a preview snippet, so make it captivating to pique curiosity. In the body of the email, get straight to the point and make your first request within the first couple of paragraphs. Include multiple calls to action throughout the email, using different phrasing or display styles like links or buttons. However, keep it focused—direct all calls to action to the same place. Avoid overwhelming recipients by asking them to donate, RSVP to an event, and register as a volunteer all in one email.

You can also take your digital fundraising offline by using quick response (QR) codes, which you can add to merchandising and offline advertising. These black and white squares have a unique pattern that can be scanned using the phone's camera app to direct users to specific digital destinations, such as websites or PDFs. Countless websites will allow you to create a unique QR code: you just need to provide your destination link.

Finally, crowdfunding is an increasingly popular tactic in digital fundraising. As mentioned in a previous chapter, crowdfunding harnesses the power of social media, crowdsourcing donations from far and wide to support a campaign. GoFundMe is one of the most well-known crowdfunding platforms, but there are many others well suited to nonprofit fundraisers including:

- **GoFundMe** is the leading crowdfunding platform. With its intuitive and user-friendly interface, it is extremely easy to use even for novices. It features excellent social sharing tools and a secure platform for online donations, with flexible payment options. It also offers features like goal tracking, updates, and donor communication tools to keep campaigners and donors engaged.
- **Crowdfunder** offers the advantage of zero fees and provides dedicated coaches to support your fundraising campaign, along with the opportunity to offer rewards and access donation matching programs.
- **TheGivingMachine** introduces innovative features such as collecting donations through

retail partners and a unique giving lottery scheme.

- **GlobalGiving** not only serves as a fundraising platform but also provides corporate partnerships, match-funding opportunities, and additional tools and training for nonprofits.
- **Givey** is great for smaller charities, particularly those based in the UK.

Take some time to explore the different crowdfunding platforms out there and look for the best one for your organization. With this wide array of crowdfunding platforms at your disposal, you can tap into the support of a global community to fuel your nonprofit's mission.

10 STEPS FOR A SUCCESSFUL DIGITAL FUNDRAISER

1. Define your goals and target audience:

Identify who you want to reach and prioritize the appropriate channels for your fundraising efforts. Follow your ideal donors and tailor your content to their interests and communication patterns.

2. Set up your nonprofit account:

Take advantage of any additional benefits you might have as a nonprofit and ensure your team understands how to maximize the platform's features.

3. Assign clear roles to all team members:

Don't assume someone will be on top of something if you don't previously agree on it. Agree on who will write, design, and publish content. Who will monitor and respond to questions or comments? Who will check your inbox periodically?

4. Create a content calendar:

Plan your posts, considering key dates and events worth leveraging in your campaign. From Mother's Day or International Women's Day to Earth Hour or World Oceans Day, there are endless dates to organize campaigns around.

5. Share compelling stories:

Highlight the people behind your mission, showcase the impact of your nonprofit, and acknowledge the generosity of donors. Make it personal: Instagram photos containing faces are 38% more likely to garner likes and 32% more likely to be commented on than those without faces (Georgia Tech, 2014). Introduce your donors and supporters to what life is like behind the scenes—show them who your staff and volunteers are and what they do. You can also share stories about the donors who have helped your cause. Acknowledge their generosity and the impact it has enabled. Invite them to share in these victories and spread the word.

6. Use visuals and interactive features:

Leverage images, videos, live streams, and interactive features on platforms like Instagram and Facebook to enhance engagement and reach a wider audience. The more interaction your content receives, the higher the chances that the platform will prioritize it for a wider audience.

7. Include clear calls to action:

Encourage followers to engage, donate, volunteer, or share your posts. Every post should have a specific call to action. Don't hesitate to invite them to take meaningful actions such as signing up, donating, or volunteering.

Additionally, empower your staff, volunteers, and partners to create their own posts or reshare your organization's content, further fueling the momentum of your campaign.

8. Partner with other organizations:

Collaborate with aligned companies or agencies to amplify your campaign's impact. Seek support from high-profile supporters or advocates to leverage their influence. Reach out to other companies or agencies that align and inquire about joining forces to amplify your campaign. And if you have any high-profile supporters or advocates who are well known in their own right, ask if they would be willing to get involved and lend their influence to your cause.

9. Be responsive and stay current:

Reply promptly to comments and messages from your followers. Stay up to date with platform trends and new features to remain relevant and stand out online.

10. Don't forget to use hashtags:

Hashtags are incredibly useful to connect with users that might not be familiar with your nonprofit. Existing relevant and popular hashtags will allow you to expand the organic reach of your posts. For example, a pet shelter might leverage hashtags like #adoptdontshop #animalrescue #animalrights #animallover, or a campaign for Black History Month might use hashtags like #blackhistorymonth or #blackhistoryfacts.

Summary

Digital platforms have transformed how we communicate, connect, and gather support for a cause. Use social media platforms, paid digital advertising, and crowdfunding platforms to harvest the global power of digital media.

In this chapter, I've introduced you to the key platforms for connecting with your audience, expanding your contacts, and engaging in effective fundraising. There's no need to be overwhelmed: take some time to analyze the different options out there and choose the right ones for you. Not every social media platform will be right for your organization, so recognize your strengths and weaknesses, and focus on the ones that will be most useful to you.

Now that you're aware of the key steps involved in planning and delivering a digital fundraiser, let's move on to explore the world of campaigns. In the next chapter, you will develop a thorough understanding of campaigning and how to engage donors and potential partners through this type of strategy.

STRATEGY #4: THE CAMPAIGN

In the realm of marketing, there is a crucial concept known as the buyer's journey, a term that refers to the path that potential customers follow from the early realization of a problem to the ultimate purchase decision. Similarly, within the context of a nonprofit, the donor's journey also starts with awareness. Without knowledge of your nonprofit's existence or the issue it tries to address, how can a potential donor decide to support your cause? Awareness stands as the cornerstone of garnering support and is the essential first step to successful fundraising.

Raising awareness is a crucial step in gaining support, and campaigns play a significant role in achieving this. While it is every communicator's dream to come up with a campaign that sets the stage ablaze and gets people talking (and donating), generating awareness is not often the result of a one-hit wonder; it's rather a captivating journey that requires sustained effort and dedication.

In this chapter, we will delve into the significance of campaigns in raising awareness and funds. By understanding the power of campaigns, you'll be equipped to attract potential donors and partners effectively.

WHAT ARE CAMPAIGNS AND WHY ARE THEY SO IMPORTANT?

In essence, these strategic endeavors are tools used by organizations and individuals to spread public awareness and foster understanding about specific issues, causes, or topics. They can also be implemented to gather economic support or rally volunteers for a cause they are already aware of. But before we delve into the different types of campaigns and how to effectively design and implement one, I want to take a few minutes to highlight their importance. Successful awareness campaigns have the ability to shape our perceptions and behaviors, and chances are you've been influenced by campaigns orchestrated by nonprofits.

Think back to 2014 when buckets of ice were raining down on people's heads—yes, the aforementioned ALS Ice Bucket Challenge. This viral sensation not only raised worldwide awareness but also generated substantial donations for amyotrophic lateral sclerosis (ALS). And if you're a bit older, you might recall the incredible combination of awareness campaigns that led to the history-making Montreal Protocol, an international agreement signed in 1987 to protect the ozone layer by phasing out the production and use of ozone-depleting substances. These examples showcase the transformative power of well-crafted awareness campaigns: not only can they unlock significant financial support for important causes, but also reshape the world.

While your work is ongoing and permanent, campaigns run for a determined time frame, potentially taking on several iterations over time to truly galvanize support. Although it may seem like you're bombarding people with the same message, the truth is that the public often needs repeated exposure for it to truly sink in.

Moreover, designing and executing an awareness campaign will enhance your nonprofit's internal dynamics. They don't just spur your donors into action but help focus your team's efforts and energy on a big vision for the future. The structure of a campaign calls for robust planning and budgeting, reinforcing your nonprofit's internal capacity, including infrastructure, systems, and technology. As your team gains campaign experience, future initiatives will run even more smoothly, harnessing the full potential of your organization.

TYPES OF FUNDRAISING CAMPAIGNS

It's very likely that at any given time, your nonprofit will be either actively campaigning or planning for a campaign. Campaigns come in a variety of shapes and sizes—beyond just raffles, walk-a-thons, or galas—and we'll dive into this diverse landscape now.

As we have already established, building public awareness is a fundamental component of any nonprofit's fundraising strategy. **Using awareness campaigns**, you can educate the public, fostering a deeper connection to the issue at stake. Think, for example, about the Earth Hour Campaign, a global environmental campaign initiated by the World Wildlife Fund (WWF) and designed to raise awareness about climate change and the need for energy conservation, or the It Gets Better Project, which was launched to support LGBTQ+ youth and combat bullying and discrimination. The more people are aware of your cause, the likelier they are to connect to support it.

Online fundraising campaigns are purely digital initiatives that leverage channels such as email, social media, and digital advertising. A digital campaign run solely on social media is referred to as a social media campaign. While they might seem cheaper to implement, as they happen solely in the digital realm, they will often require impactful videos or interactive content, and have an allocated budget to expand its reach. Likewise, an email campaign focuses on leveraging the power of email marketing, potentially incorporating crowdfunding elements to harness the collective power of online networks and secure numerous small donations. Think, for example, about the emails politicians send during elections, asking supporters to contribute through donations. Additionally, individuals can also create their own personal fundraising campaigns, known as peer-to-peer fundraising, tapping into their personal networks to rally support for your cause.

A text-to-give campaign is a simple campaign that enables donors to give to a cause by sending a text message to their cell phone. Keep in mind, potential donors will most likely only engage with a text-to-give campaign if it's around an issue they are already aware of.

Campaigns based around direct marketing tactics, such as door-to-door visits, phone calls, or even direct mail, demand more resources and effort, though the personal touch they offer can make a significant impact.

Membership campaigns focus on converting prospects into donors and increasing contribution levels by building stronger relationships with them. By positioning supporters as members, they feel a greater sense of involvement in the cause, leading to increased loyalty. A supporter who considers themselves a member will feel more involved in a cause and is more likely to give, more often—even if only when their annual membership renewal rolls around.

Capital campaigns are designed to secure major gifts and have the aim of raising a significant sum within a defined timeframe. In most cases, capital campaigns are intended to fund big projects such as renovations or new purchases. For example, your nonprofit might start a crowdfunding campaign to build a school in a foreign country. Typically, these campaigns begin with a quiet phase, during which your team approaches key donors for substantial contributions, which will make up the core funding of your project. This phase tends to require dedicated efforts in research and relationship-building. The subsequent public phase marks the official announcement of the campaign, inviting contributions from a broader audience.

Comprehensive or integrated campaigns can span multiple categories and give people different options to support your organization's diverse needs and be part of something greater. These campaigns can also serve as an opportunity to re-engage with lapsed donors. This type of campaign requires coordination to present a united front to the public. For example, a nonprofit may simultaneously fundraise for a building project and run an annual campaign, allowing major donors to contribute to both initiatives, with the first campaign that reaches out potentially receiving their full support.

9 STEPS TO ORGANIZE SUCCESSFUL FUNDRAISING CAMPAIGNS

Embarking on a successful fundraising campaign requires careful planning and execution. If you're ready to make a difference, follow these essential steps to design and optimize your campaign for success:

1. Choose a campaign type and identify your target audience:

Who does your nonprofit want to reach? Let this knowledge guide your selection of key campaigning channels. If direct mail has brought you success, weave it into your marketing strategy. If digital channels have been your golden ticket, focus your efforts there.

2. Craft a compelling message:

What do you want your audience to know? Design a key message or messages that will shine throughout your campaign. Make it resonate, stay consistent, and speak directly to the hearts of your supporters.

3. Assess your resources and set a budget and timeframe:

Be realistic and strategic. How much can you invest in this campaign, and how much do you aim to raise? Evaluate your resources, plan a fixed campaign budget, and make thoughtful estimates for expenses and revenue. Strike a balance in timing. Give your campaign enough time to gather momentum and attract donations but avoid donor fatigue by not stretching it too long.

4. Measure success with impact:

Identify metrics that will help you gauge the effectiveness of your campaign. How will you measure the impact you're making? Regularly check these metrics and be ready to adjust your strategy along the way if needed.

5. Harness the power of storytelling:

Breathe life into your campaign. Refine your overarching message and craft a succinct narrative that captures attention. Keep your campaign messaging clear and focused. Share impactful stories that put faces to your cause. For instance, meet Nisha, a 12-year-old whose dreams of education are hindered by a lack of access to period care products. Use Nisha's story to show how girls like her are missing out on essential education. Let people see how their donations can change lives and create a brighter future: provide specific examples, such as "just $100 a year will ensure one of her classmates can attend class year-round so she doesn't fall behind on learning." Even more than numbers, personal stories bring a mission to life—showing how someone's life can change. People give to other people, and because of people.

6. Ignite the promotion:

Get people's attention. This is particularly true for digital fundraisers when you want to generate captivating content that reflects the nature of your campaign. It's not business as usual, so ensure your online presence reflects that. Dial up the activity, create buzz, and make it easy to donate. Test your donation process rigorously to ensure a seamless experience. Any glitches at all will lead users to give up and click away. Enable both single and ongoing donations, while reminding the public of the value of recurring donors. If you are working with influencers or encouraging individuals to create their own personal fundraisers, supply them with information and assets so that they represent your nonprofit accurately and consistently.

7. Integrate online and offline elements:

If you have in-person activities, ensure a consistent experience across all touch points. Align messaging and tone across channels. If there are offline elements in your campaign, such as live events, door knocking, etc., ensure all team members are aligned on goals and expectations. A donor who experiences the campaign across different touch points should have a seamless experience that is consistent with the organization they have come to know.

8. Keep the momentum going:

As the campaign nears its end, step up your efforts. As the campaign reaches its end period, it might be tempting to ease off, but this is often the time to step up your efforts. If you are making your fundraising goal public, regularly update how far you are from reaching your goal and maintain a countdown to show the remaining time for people to contribute. People tend to leave things until the last minute and many generous donations come in just before the clock runs out when they feel they have the power to make or break your campaign.

9. A heartfelt finale:

Wrap up the campaign with a big thank you to everyone involved. Remember, fundraising is a collective effort, and appreciation goes a long way.

Summary

The focused, sustained, and time-limited effort behind a campaign will boost any fundraising strategy, raising awareness and rallying support toward your cause. This chapter has shown you the power of campaigns for nonprofits and guided you through the most important steps to implement a successful campaign.

Think about your own campaigns. Are you currently planning one? Do you have one up and running? Analyze your current efforts through the lens of the information

I've provided you with and don't be afraid to change course if you see room for improvement.

In the next chapter, we'll shift gears and tackle the fifth fundraising strategy I want to share with you: annual giving.

8

STRATEGY #5: ANNUAL GIVING

"We need to value donors as much as we need value from them."

— REINIER SPRUIT

When crafting your nonprofit's fundraising strategy, it's crucial to recognize the foundational role of annual giving. This ongoing and organized effort throughout the year allows donors to contribute multiple times, making it more than just a one-time gift. Unlike targeted campaigns or one-time donations, annual giving provides a reliable and consistent source of funding that supports day-to-day operations, sustains vital programs, and covers essential operating expenses.

Sometimes nonprofits overlook the significance of annual giving, focusing more on flashy campaigns. However, if you hope to keep things running, it's essential to acknowledge that annual giving is what keeps your organization running. It forms the backbone of your budget and ensures the sustainability of your programs and services.

In this chapter, I will show you the importance of annual giving and guide you in establishing a robust protocol that keeps the funds flowing consistently throughout the year. By understanding and prioritizing annual giving, you can build a solid foundation for your nonprofit's financial stability and long-term success.

WHY IS ANNUAL GIVING SO IMPORTANT FOR NONPROFITS?

1. Financial Stability:

Annual giving provides a reliable and steady source of income. By cultivating a broad base of regular donors, your organization will be able to generate consistent funding to support ongoing operations and programs. Stability is key if you hope to plan and budget effectively and is what makes work possible year after year. While grants or government funds may dry up, a strong network of reliable donors can keep an organization afloat and thriving even when things get hard.

2. Donor Engagement and Retention:

Regular contact and communication with supporters and donors are key to creating the sense of connection that makes annual giving possible. By keeping your donors updated on the impact of their contributions, you can strengthen loyalty and retain them over the long term.

3. Flexibility and Responsiveness:

Unlike funds raised through restricted campaigns, annual giving funds can be directed wherever they are most needed. Nonprofits can allocate these funds to cover operational expenses, invest in new initiatives, address emerging challenges, or fill gaps in underfunded areas. This flexibility enables organizations to adapt and respond to evolving needs and opportunities.

4. Mission Reinforcement:

Annual giving campaigns serve as powerful platforms to showcase and reinforce your nonprofit's mission and impact. The type of communication required by annual giving allows you to place the organization's core work in the spotlight.

5. Donor Benefits:

Annual giving offers tangible benefits for donors as well. Many countries provide tax deductions or incentives for charitable donations, making annual giving an attractive option for those seeking to maximize their philanthropic impact while reaping the potential financial benefits.

TYPES OF ANNUAL FUND PROGRAMS

Year-end fundraising, also known as the giving season, holds tremendous potential for nonprofits. In December alone, approximately one-third of annual giving occurs, and approximately 10% happens in a flurry during the last three days of the year (Donorbox, 2022). As people spend time giving gifts, spending time with family, and enjoying a renewed sense of community, they also feel inspired to give. Moreover, it's the final opportunity to make tax-deductible contributions for the calendar year. Plan well in advance to make the most of the year-end fundraising—even as early as in the previous quarter. Competition is fierce during this time, so you need to choose and disseminate compelling messaging. Make sure it's aligned with your broader mission, reinforcing your nonprofit's purpose and values. For example, a nonprofit focused on education may choose to highlight the transformative power of gifting educational resources to underprivileged children during the holiday season.

Sustainer programs are designed to cultivate long-term relationships with donors who commit to regular support, whether through monthly, quarterly, or other recurring contributions. With the convenience of automatic giving options like bank transfers, credit or debit cards, and workplace giving, becoming a sustainer has never been easier. These donors are among the most loyal supporters in your database and form the ideal bedrock for an annual fund. A sustainer program can take various approaches, such as converting one-time donors into recurring givers or encouraging existing donors to increase the frequency or amount of their contributions. Don't forget to provide incentives for increased participation. For example, a nonprofit focused on environmental conservation might provide access to behind-the-scenes footage or cute memes featuring the animals protected by the organization.

Viral fundraising initiatives harness the power of social media to create campaigns that spread rapidly and gain momentum. Since your nonprofit will appeal to donors throughout the year, keeping things fresh and engaging is key, finding new and innovative ways to capture their attention and inspire action. There's no guarantee that a campaign will go viral: sometimes the most well-thought-out campaigns can fall flat, while simple ones just ignite a spark. However, it's essential to remember that any piece of content has the potential to gain traction. Invest in quality communication materials, particularly videos, which can significantly amplify your annual giving efforts. For example, if your nonprofit is an animal rescue operation, you could create a heartwarming video showing the before and after of the animals you help save.

12 STEPS TO SUCCESSFULLY FUNDRAISE WITH ANNUAL INCENTIVES

Annual giving campaigns are just as pivotal a part of running a successful and sustainable nonprofit as capital and awareness campaigns are. After all, these programs are what make keeping the lights on possible. They pay for staff salaries, underfunded priorities, and daily expenses. So now that you're aware of their importance, let's dive into how to execute an engaging and successful annual giving initiative.

1. Set your goal:

All successful campaigns start with a clear target in mind and annual giving campaigns are no exception. Determine the amount you need and track your progress throughout the year. If this is your first annual giving venture, review last year's expenditure as a starting point. While you may not be aiming to cover all operating expenses, this will provide a benchmark to move forward.

2. Plan for success:

Once you have your annual goal set, break it down into smaller milestones. Consider dividing them by quarter or month. Timing is key: map out your annual fundraising efforts over the year, remembering how essential December is for fundraising. Be aware of any other campaigns by your nonprofit and draw a flexible plan that can be revised as the year progresses. Think beyond this year: a solid plan can be reused over and over again, saving time and energy.

3. Strategize and segment:

Determine the assets, resources, and channels you will need for your campaign. Will you be using traditional marketing avenues, digital outreach, or a mix of both? Consider developing targeted campaigns for specific segments like one-off donors, lapsed donors, young or elderly donors, and so on. You'll gain valuable data and insights into your donors' preferences. Keep in mind consistency: any segmented campaign should seamlessly integrate with the messaging in all others.

4. Research:

Analyze your current prospects so you can optimize your fundraising efforts. Identify and prioritize individuals who are most likely to have the resources and inclination to make significant contributions. Remember that major gifts can sometimes account for the majority of your funding. Don't forget about lapsed donors, as they could just need a nudge to re-engage. Personalize your communication and customize your asks accordingly. Keeping an updated database with as much information as possible is essential.

5. Recruit and organize your dream team:

Annual giving campaigns demand dedicated teams. Distribute responsibilities among them, focusing on the high-potential prospects you identified in the previous steps. Provide them with the tools they need to succeed.

Your annual giving initiative will likely encompass direct asks, marketing and outreach, and events. Consider recruiting volunteers and assign your experienced staffers as supervisors and coordinators. Don't forget to create a contingency plan to handle potential staff changes or leaves.

6. Craft compelling appeals:

It's now time to create impactful and compelling appeals that resonate with your prospects and donors. Utilize various channels, such as electronic or direct email, phone calls, and face-to-face conversations. Integrate your various marketing channels consistently but find creative ways to use each complementary so they don't feel repetitive. Harness the power of emotional story-telling to make your fundraiser come to life. Consider tying your appeals to key dates or occasions to add a sense of urgency. Maintain regular communication throughout the year, but up your game in December: it's a busy and competitive month but can yield great results.

7. Nurture major donor relationships:

Face-to-face requests often occur at the end of culti-vating major donors. Approach these requests with care. A face-to-face ask should never come as a surprise. It should be the natural next step, an extension of previous communications and touch points. Nurture these special relationships: engage your existing donors, considering their giving history, personal background, and indicators of wealth. Tailor your engagement accordingly.

8. Monitor and optimize:

Regularly check your campaign metrics to track progress toward your overall goal. Assess the performance of individual campaign items, like specific advertisements, newsletters, videos, etc. Don't be afraid to tinker with something that's not working or dropping an unsuccessful strategy that's consuming energy and resources. Optimize your strategy based on data and testing. While it's beneficial to improve upon a base blueprint each year, inject excitement by introducing surprises. Keep your campaign fresh, interesting, and engaging.

9. Optimize the donation process:

Donating should be a seamless and fast experience. Your online donation platform should be user-friendly and optimized with sharing buttons. Not everyone will know how much to give. Provide preset donation levels while allowing for custom donations. Highlight the impact of each level and emphasize the importance of annual giving.

10. Engage your donors:

Inform donors about the impact of their contribution: this is particularly important for first-time donors. If the donation is substantial, a call or handwritten note is a good idea. Seek their input and feedback to make them feel valued. Follow up in the upcoming weeks or months, emphasizing key dates such as the anniversary of their gift. This will build rapport and trust—the key to nurturing long-term giving relationships.

11. Promote recurring giving:

Retaining donors is easier than attracting new ones. Encourage recurring giving options with strategies such as a simple tick box on a form, a PS in a written communication, an actionable button in your newsletter, or a follow-up ask. Consider offering perks or benefits to regular supporters, who make up the core of your donor base. It could be a membership program with various tiers based on giving level or longevity. Brainstorm ways to show recognition, fostering a sense of belonging which will translate into a habit of giving. Access to exclusive content, merchandise, or special events is always appealing. Capture pledges from donors who commit to future contributions, creating guidelines to secure additional funds. These may be unconditional or contingent on the nonprofit meeting certain conditions.

12. Explore business support:

Don't overlook the potential of corporate support. Start with low-hanging fruit—businesses with an existing connection to your nonprofit. Make use of any connections your staff or board members may have and recruit your top supporters to help you make new contacts. Seek companies that are aligned to your mission and core values and tap into their corporate social responsibility budgets. Understand their budget cycles, priorities, and expectations for charitable partnerships. Refer to the partnerships chapter for a refresher.

Summary

Annual giving is the backbone of your fundraising efforts, providing you a chance to showcase your mission. Tackle these campaigns through the various channels available, such as events, meetings, phone calls, direct mail, and digital media. While annual giving campaigns require significant time and resources, the payoff is worth it: increased awareness and visibility of your cause, donor acquisition, enhanced donor participation, and invaluable insights into what inspires and resonates with the public. As you've learned, strike the delicate balance between integrating and segmenting your multiple channels and campaigns.

This chapter has taught you about the importance of developing a strategic, long-term approach to day-to-day operations, keeping options open for your nonprofit throughout the year.

Think about your own annual giving fundraising efforts: Are you keeping your database updated? Do you have devoted team members? Do you have a yearly plan that's easy to update? Revise your own processes and improve them following the guidelines I've provided. Let's now shift gears and explore the key elements for hosting a successful fundraising event.

9

STRATEGY #6: EVENT HOSTING

When people think of fundraising for nonprofits, events are often what immediately comes to mind. While they are often seen as the highlight of fundraising, the reality is that planning and executing a successful event requires a tremendous amount of effort. And the reality is that even with substantial budgeting planning, even experienced event planners can struggle to achieve a reasonable profit.

There's just no way around it: hosting events is not for the faint of heart. However, with proper organization, they can be simpler to pull off than you might expect—as well as being very rewarding, both financially and to your organization. Whether dinners, galas, auctions, tournaments, car washes, concerts, cook-offs, or carnivals, successful events can become so renowned that they overshadow the organizations themselves, like the case of March of Dimes, which changed its name to align with its prominent fundraising event. Events bring people together, attracting new donors and partners, and rekindling existing support. The group setting reduces the pressure typically associated with face-to-face solicitations while maintaining a personal connection by putting names to faces in real life. Moreover, they are enjoyable and exciting to existing members, fostering a sense of belonging and community. When combined with a well-executed PR strategy, an event can significantly enhance an organization's profile. Event organizers can align events with their fundraising calendar, facilitating staff and volunteer engagement, collaboration, and celebration at the conclusion of a campaign. If your organization deals with urgent needs, such as emergency responses to natural disasters, events can be the natural way to go.

This chapter will provide you with a straightforward strategy to organize successful events, which you can easily tailor to your unique circumstances. With these guidelines, you will be well equipped to host your next event, raising awareness, garnering community support, and securing funding for your mission.

TYPES OF FUNDRAISING EVENTS

Fundraising events can be categorized into two main types:

1. Events that are specific to your organization and target individuals already invested in your cause. These events clearly communicate attendees will be asked to make donations and often have a fixed amount.

2. Community-oriented events, where fundraising is incorporated at the start, with participants paying to participate. Think of bake sales or sporting events, which will leave attendees with a positive experience and predispose them to spread the word. If your organization is on the smaller size, fun runs or walks are easy to plan and organize, while concerts and live events are better suited for organizations with larger budgets (Finch, 2015).

Short of ideas on what to organize? Here are some of my favorites, along with some caveats to consider before embarking on one :

Galas are large-scale fundraisers often hosted by nonprofits once a year as a signature event. They typically include dinner, entertainment, and a raffle or auction. Planning a gala requires substantial time and upfront investment, including scouting facilities, arranging MCs, planning menus, and organizing presentations. Funds are raised through ticket sales, either individual tickets or entire tables, and sometimes through sponsorships. Since they can be expensive, they tend to be the domain of larger nonprofits. Things like catering costs, staff requirements, rental and venue fees, as well as the costs of promoting and marketing the event can quickly add up. However, the average return is also generally higher when compared to other types of events.

As I mentioned, while **auctions** can be part of a gala event, they can also be standalone fundraising events. In an auction, items are sold to the highest bidder, and nonprofits often solicit donated goods from businesses to auction off. Depending on the scale, a lot may go into planning an auction, or it may be relatively low effort. You can organize an online-only auction through a platform that handles bids, notifies winners, and manages logistics on your behalf—however, be aware that they will generally take a cut.

A twist on the traditional auction is the **silent auction**. Goods are displayed for inspection, and attendees write down their bids. Mystery boxes or bags are a clever way to add intrigue and excitement to the auction by combining smaller items.

Marathons are popular and versatile fundraising events for your community. They don't have to be strenuous: walk-a-thons, dance-a-thons, golf-a-thons, or bike-a-thons are usually fun, family affairs. They also have the lowest cost per dollar raised ratio (Finch, 2015), delivering the most bang for your buck. Planning a marathon event requires minimal effort, making them the perfect type of fundraising event for smaller teams and nonprofits. Participants raise funds by seeking sponsorships from their personal and professional networks, often fostering friendly competition. Donations can come from anywhere in the world, not just from the event's location. Your nonprofit will often be responsible for organizing prizes and sponsors, managing sign-ups, providing encouragement, tracking results, and potentially hosting a celebration after the event.

Online fundraising events are a great complement and can even replace in-person events. These include crowdfunding challenges, virtual game nights, concerts, workshops, or trivia nights. Organizing an online event is typically less resource-intensive compared to live events, as you can utilize technology that your nonprofit already uses. Online events also tend to be more inclusive and accessible, as you can include features like closed captions, transcripts, and screen reader accommodations, which might be particularly important—depending on the work of your organization. Virtual a-thon events allow participants worldwide to take part at their convenience and can span several days or even weeks—unlike in-person events. Add an element of competition to increase the participants' commitment to the campaign. The ultimate goal is to collect donations through your website, ensuring a smooth and seamless process.

Art exhibits can be relatively easy to plan, although they are better suited for mid-sized or larger nonprofits. A charitable art show can take the form of a competition where artists pay an entry fee to showcase their work for judging. Prizes for the winners can be donated by local businesses. Alternatively, you can recruit artists to display their work for sale, with a percentage of sales being donated to your nonprofit. Inviting well-known artists can attract more interest and maximize the potential success of your art exhibit fundraiser.

Sporting events also serve as effective fundraisers for nonprofits. You could simply set up a concession stall at a local football, basketball, or baseball game, and offer snacks and drinks, taking home a percentage of the sales. The atmosphere at a stadium is typically spirited and communal, which can foster donations. However, while these events can be fun, the return on investment may not be as strong. Another option is to organize a tournament or host a fun run/walk. Consider partnering with a local team to auction off their time, allowing people to bid for individuals or the entire team. Local athletes could also donate their time for various activities, from chores to running a fitness class. All proceeds go toward your nonprofit under this scheme.

Lastly, **donor appreciation events** are held to express gratitude, highlight the impact of donor support, and strengthen donor relationships. These events are free for attending donors, focusing on building rapport and suggesting other ways advocates can contribute without a direct ask for monetary donations.

13 STEPS TO HOSTING A SUCCESSFUL EVENT

Hosting a successful fundraising event requires careful planning and execution. Mid to large nonprofits have an advantage when it comes to hosting events, thanks to their bigger budgets and diverse teams. Nevertheless, and even if your organization is small and/or new to the world of event planning, following these key steps will help you achieve a strong return on investment and make it a success:

1. Form a planning and hosting committee:

Establish a main team responsible for executing the event and create subcommittees that will handle different aspects of the fundraiser, such as production, promotion, and fundraising. Collaborate closely to ensure seamless coordination and execution. Establish a planning committee, charged with behind-the-scenes tasks, and a host committee, which will focus on fundraising and donor recruitment. You should also have an event day committee that's responsible for the big day itself.

2. Define the purpose and goals:

Determine the main purpose of your fundraiser, whether it's increasing visibility, raising funds, or thanking supporters. Choose an event type, date, and budget that aligns with your goals. Consider the audience, mission, fundraising targets, available resources, and expertise when deciding on the event type. This can help you decide what will make for a compelling event and your metrics for success.

3. Build an event budget and timeline:

Develop a rough outline of the event budget and create a project timeline. These will evolve over time, but having a preliminary plan will provide a foundation for organizing the event.

4. Research costs and suppliers:

Identify the requirements for your event and research potential costs and suppliers. This includes securing a venue, setting a theme, arranging for decor, consumables, entertainment, photographers, and other necessary elements. Consider your target audience and their interests, as well as your fundraising goal and budget. It's great to shoot for the stars, but don't run before you can walk—work your way up to that annual gala.

5. Recruit sponsors and partners:

Reach out to potential sponsors and partners to support your event. Tailor your outreach to each organization, highlighting the benefits they will receive from supporting your cause. Any additional funding or gifts you are able to line up at this stage will ensure your budget stretches as far as possible. For example, if you are planning a charity run, you could ask a sporting goods store to sponsor the event and potentially provide some athletic gear for prizes.

6. Plan, plan, plan:

Plan and organize your event to the very last details. The list is long and includes securing a location and setting a theme, then tackling décor, consumables, entertainment, and photographers, among others. Remember that high-profile performers or professionals may have a busy schedule, so contact them early. Check with local regulation and food compliance norms. Virtual events usually don't have so many items, but you will still need to plan. Adapt engagement techniques for virtual platforms, such as icebreakers, polls, quizzes, and breakout chat rooms. Break down all considerations into categories to ensure nothing is overlooked.

7. Get people talking:

It's now time to promote the event. Design and deploy promotional materials both physical and digital, including posters, flyers, social media graphics, emails, web pages, and forms. As you start promoting the event through your marketing channels, you can also reach out to local media to expand your target audience and encourage partners, sponsors, staff, volunteers, and advocates to spread the word.

8. Organize volunteers:

Recruit volunteers to help with the event. From selling tickets or enlisting participants through to cleaning up after the event itself, enthusiastic volunteers are essential. Assign roles for ticket sales, participant management, event setup, attendee assistance, and post-event cleanup.

9. Conduct a dress rehearsal:

Schedule a dry run to practice ahead of time to ensure everything is running smoothly between staff, volunteers, vendors, and anyone else involved. Create a detailed playbook for the event, listing each step and responsible individuals.

10. Use the event as an engagement opportunity:

Emphasize your nonprofit's mission and provide opportunities for attendees to understand how they can help beyond the immediate fundraising goal. This is a great time to request annual pledges and consolidate long-term commitments. Provide progress reports throughout the event and try to gather additional support to reach your goal.

11. Follow up and say thanks:

The work doesn't end when everyone leaves. As I've said over and over throughout this book, promoting long-term relationships with your donors is essential. Share post-event updates on social media, thanking participants and donors. Send personalized thank you letters acknowledging their attendance and generosity. Don't forget to ask for feedback: donors like to feel like they have a say in the future of the nonprofit. Cultivate a long-term connection with attendees: almost a third of offline-only, first-time donors are retained for more than a year, which is slightly higher than 25% of online-only new donors (Double the Donation, 2022).

12. Evaluate and debrief:

Take stock of the event afterward—calculate the total funds raised, expenses, attendance, and net profit. Depending on the size of your organization and events, you might choose to organize the information in a basic spreadsheet or pay for specific software designed for fundraising and event management. This investment will make things easier in the future. Run a debrief with your committees to review the event's success and areas for improvement.

13. Acknowledge event contributors:

Recognize and appreciate everyone involved and make sure to pay any outstanding debts with providers. Give special thanks to the event coordinator, who would have held the most stressful position of all, for their significant role and dedication.

Summary

Events are one of the best ways to foster connection, raise substantial funds, and build a community with your donors and supporters. They are a high-effort but a potentially high-return way to raise awareness and money, and many nonprofits have developed a reputation for hosting impactful, profitable, long-running events.

In this chapter, you've learned about the various types of fundraising events and how to organize a successful one. Remember to capitalize on the momentum your fundraising event creates. Continue to engage with new and renewed contacts and nurture your relationship with them over time.

Think about the events you've organized in the past and recognize room for improvement where possible. Assess your capabilities and strengths as a nonprofit and organize the right type of event for you. As I have explained, bigger is not always better. Begin by testing the water and move toward larger and more demanding events.

In the next chapter, I will explore the final fundraising strategy in this book. We will focus on the significance of donor retention and the strategies involved in cultivating sustainable long-term giving relationships. Donor retention is a crucial aspect of fundraising, as maintaining existing donors tends to be more cost-effective and efficient compared to acquiring new ones. By building strong relationships with donors and fostering their continued support, organizations can ensure ongoing financial stability and make a greater impact on their missions.

10

STRATEGY #7: DONOR RETENTION AND MANAGEMENT

"The manner of giving is worth more than the gift."

— PIERRE CORNEILLE

Just as customers are the lifeblood of a business, donors are what keep a nonprofit afloat. For any charitable organization, loyal and consistent supporters who donate regularly are invaluable. But these kinds of relationships don't just spring up out of nowhere. Cultivating such relationships requires effort and dedication from you and your staff. Building trust and nurturing the seeds of a mutually beneficial long-term relationship is an ongoing process that is essential to the survival of any nonprofit.

Strong donor retention is essential for an organization's financial health and stability. It enables your nonprofit to plan more effectively by providing predictable income, which facilitates accurate forecasting and budgeting from year to year. A higher donor retention rate also means a larger donor database to work with and more prospects for planning major campaigns or soliciting significant contributions.

In this chapter, I will delve into the importance of donor retention and share with you some key steps to ensure you will keep your donors happy. If you've ever struggled with planning and budgeting or have felt the burnout of constantly having to acquire new donors, then this is the right chapter for you.

WHAT IS DONOR RETENTION AND WHY DOES IT MATTER?

We'll define donor retention as the number or percentage of donors who continue giving to your nonprofit, as opposed to those who stop after their initial gift. You can calculate your donor retention rate by dividing the number of repeat donors this year by the number of people who donated last year. For example, if you have 220 donors in a single year and only 79 out of those give again in the following period, then your donor retention rate would be 36%.

A higher retention rate means maintaining a consistent supporter base year after year, reducing the pressure to continually acquire new donors. This is key because, in reality, many organizations either lose money or barely break even on the first donation from a new donor.

The value of a newly acquired donor lies not only in the immediate gift but also in unlocking long-term giving potential. If you manage to secure a second donation, often referred to as the golden donation, the likelihood of retaining that donor on an ongoing basis significantly improves. Not only does it cost less to keep a donor than to find a new one, but previous donors are also more likely to give more. Their initial donation is rarely their largest, and as their affinity toward your cause deepens, they are more likely to contribute in significant ways. Major gifts, in particular, are the result of a lasting long-term relationship. Long-term donors may also volunteer at events, join your board, or spread the word about your mission without prompting.

So what's a good retention rate? Nonprofits have an average donor retention rate of about 45%, although it's worth noting that retention rates for new donors are even lower, around 30% (Bloomerang, 2022). No organization is entirely immune to attrition or losing donors. It is unrealistic to expect a 100% retention rate. That's why it is so crucial to balance donor acquisition efforts with donor retention initiatives.

Ignoring donor retention may not seem like a problem in the short term, but it is a mistake that will hurt in the long run. As your donor pool shrinks over time, so do the dollars. Even a seemingly small fluctuation in your donor retention rate can represent significant losses in donations. And, unfortunately, once someone stops giving, the chances of them returning are slim.

DONOR STEWARDSHIP

Donor stewardship refers to the process of developing and nurturing a relationship with a donor after their initial gift. Stewardship means to supervise or take care of and that is exactly what your nonprofit is doing: stewarding each donor, with the ultimate goal of encouraging them to give again. Donor stewardship also involves attending to simple yet essential tasks, like properly stewarding a donor's personal information—keeping their details secure, processing their gifts correctly, and directing those funds toward the purpose the donor expected the money to go toward.

Donors want to feel appreciated and know that their contributions make a difference. But they are more than their gifts; they are also potential advocates for your mission. Your role is to create a compelling donor experience that makes them feel like an integral part of a special mission or community, encouraging them to give repeatedly and stay connected to your nonprofit. The worst-case scenario is when donors fall into the "out-of-sight, out-of-mind" category. Donors often lapse because of factors like lack of acknowledgment or lack of ongoing communication—two very preventable mistakes.

It is crucial to have a clear process in place not only for what happens immediately after someone donates but also for the subsequent information that is sent to them and when it is sent. A donor stewardship program should include recognition, relationship building, managing gifts according to donor intentions, and reporting back on the impact of their contribution. As you can see and as with all relationships in life, it all comes back to communication.

Keep your donors informed about your organization's work, outcomes, and how they can continue to engage and contribute. Acknowledge the impact their support has on your charity's mission and offer various avenues for involvement beyond monetary contributions. Remember that someone's capacity to give may fluctuate over time as their life circumstances change.

While it is great to move a donor up the value ladder—that is, increasing the size of their gifts—not everyone is in a position to give more. There are numerous ways, beyond financial support, through which individuals can contribute to a cause. Ensure your donors are aware of these options and invite them to get involved beyond their wallets and credit cards. People are donating to your organization because they believe in the cause you support: provide them with opportunities to be more involved. Embrace these ebbs and flows, as donor stewardship is not a strictly linear process.

It should go without saying, but not all of your communications should involve requests for donations. Make it clear that you care about more than just financial contributions. Create various communication channels and leverage them to establish multiple touch points, whether through direct mail, digital platforms, text messages, or phone calls. Engaging donors through these channels helps them feel connected, seen, and heard—essential steps in cultivating loyal supporters.

Lastly, I want to emphasize that donor stewardship is not a process that should be confined to isolated silos but integrated into your nonprofit's broader communication strategy. For example, if a donor has just received a thank you message, rather than immediately sending them information about your latest fundraising campaign, it may be more appropriate to wait or inform them about a different aspect, such as your upcoming major event. If your nonprofit has different departments or a number of people in charge of sending out communications, you must ensure a delicate balance and coordination so that all messages are well-timed and strategic.

Implementing effective donor stewardship may seem daunting, particularly for smaller organizations. However, small nonprofits must prioritize donor retention as well. In fact, stewarding a smaller donor base is often more manageable than managing a larger one. If you are new to stewardship, read on for a straightforward plan you can start to roll out right away.

11 STEPS TO MAINTAINING DONOR RETENTION

Developing and implementing a structured approach to donor retention is essential for your nonprofit to maintain consistency in your efforts, even when team members change over time. These are proven steps to establish a successful and enduring donor retention program:

1. Assign a dedicated team:

Expecting staff to fit these tasks in whenever they can means they will likely fall between the cracks. Designate specific individuals or at least one person in a smaller nonprofit to focus on donor relations. Additionally, consider investing in donor management software to streamline retention initiatives and ensure accurate data management. Technology can automate simple, repetitive tasks, ensure accuracy, and reduce human error, ultimately helping your team focus on and achieve your goals.

2. Evaluate your retention rate:

Assess how long your existing donors typically continue to support your organization. Lapsing donors are like funding leaks, impacting your organization's financial stability. By improving retention, you will enhance your nonprofit's bottom line. And without tracking it, you won't improve.

3. Plan your retention program:

Define your strategy for engaging donors. Outline the frequency, type, and channels of communication that will create an ideal donor experience. Research (Bloomerang, 2022) suggests that making phone contact within 90 days improves retention rates and the likelihood of receiving a second donation, often referred to as the "golden donation." Ask your trusted donors and supporters how they feel about your follow-up communication and look for areas for improvement.

4. Personalize donor outreach:

Segment your donor database into key groups such as major donors, long-time donors, lapsed donors, and new donors. Tailor your communications to each segment based on their preferences and interests. Begin the conversation by asking about their well-being and take the time to get to know them. Find out how they heard about your organization, why they were drawn to it, and why they chose to give. Record this information, so you can revisit the topics you discussed in conversation.

5. Say thanks:

Express gratitude for their support, acknowledge their contributions, and connect their donations to your nonprofit's larger mission. Highlight upcoming events, campaigns, and opportunities for involvement, and extend an invitation to stay engaged.

6. Create a welcome kit:

Develop a digital or physical welcome kit to nurture the donor relationship. While a physical one can feel more personal and can help them express their support offline as well, an electronic version will be easier to automate. Welcome them to your family of supporters; make them feel part of a thriving community. Your welcome kit can include past newsletters, educational material about your cause, and resources that can help them become effective advocates. Design shareable social media graphics to make it easy for donors to spread the word about your organization. Invite them to participate in your upcoming initiatives and share your calendar to date.

7. Maintain high-value communications:

Regularly send personalized communications to maintain strong donor relations. Let donors witness the impact of their gifts by framing their contributions as crucial to achieving your nonprofit's mission. Provide updates on your nonprofit's work, volunteer opportunities, events, and reports to deepen the relationship. Emphasize the specific outcomes and express gratitude on their behalf. If you have reached a milestone as an organization, share it with your donors. For instance, rather than stating *"We provided food and vaccinations for 10 rescue dogs thanks to your donation,"* phrase it as *"Your generous gift provided food and vaccinations for these 10 rescue dogs. On their behalf, thank you for your support."* The more specific, the better.

8. Respect their time:

Balance keeping them informed while respecting their time and privacy by allowing donors to select their communication preferences. Lots of people unsubscribe from newsletters because they feel overwhelmed: don't overdo it. If you see supporters and donors unsubscribing from your communications, it's time to reassess content and strategy. Allow them to choose how often they would like to hear from you, so they feel they're in control of communications.

9. Show genuine care and appreciation:

Demonstrate that your organization values donors as individuals by providing tokens of gratitude. Feature donors on your website, dedicate social media posts to highlight their generosity, or create videos showcasing the impact of their donations. Celebrate milestones such as birthdays or anniversaries with personalized cards or notes. Make the time to personally reach out to high-value, recurring donors with a handwritten note or phone call.

10. Foster a sense of community:

Organize events specifically dedicated to recognizing and appreciating donors. Use these events to connect with donors personally, learn more about their interests and motivations, and express gratitude face-to-face. These events also foster a sense of community among donors, allowing them to connect with one another. Use the opportunity to share a high-impact video or speech about your work and the impact of their donations. Some organizations find that running some type of membership, society, or club is also an effective way to create a community. Typically, members give time or money in exchange for certain insider benefits such as early access to information, merchandise, or exclusive events.

11. Measure and adapt:

Continually evaluate the success of your retention program and make necessary adjustments. Monitor metrics such as email open rates and the percentage of donors who volunteer. Use the data to inform decision-making and improve key performance indicators. Aim for consistent retention rates while striving for improvement.

Summary

Donor retention is an important indicator of financial health and stability. Bringing in new donors takes a lot of effort, time, and resources, so don't waste them. As I've emphasized before, investing in keeping donors happy and emotionally involved will pay off financially. While it may seem like a lot of work, the rewards are worth it.

To ensure your success, it is imperative to focus on developing a robust donor stewardship program. Take a moment to evaluate your current approach: are you methodically examining this process step by step, or are you simply improvising? Review the steps I have provided and assign specific responsibilities within your organization. Regular and strategic communication plays a pivotal role in establishing connections, fostering trust, and cultivating loyalty—the foundation of a mutually satisfying donor relationship. Your ultimate objective should be to engage each donor meaningfully and personally. In the next chapter, we will address the most common questions related to nonprofit fundraising.

11

THE FUNDRAISING FAQ

"Giving is not just about making a donation, it's about making a difference."

— KATHY CALVIN

If you have read this far, fully immersing yourself in the preceding chapters, you will have developed a solid understanding of the seven fundraising strategies I recommend. You will have a clear view of the nuances of the donor-charity relationship and how to consistently nurture givers through a variety of means. Let's round off by answering some of the top questions commonly asked when it comes to the mechanisms of nonprofit fundraising.

HOW DO YOU ASK FOR DONATIONS?

There are many ways you can ask prospective donors to give to your cause. In this book, we've covered seven major strategies that organizations of any size and type can use to their benefit. Nonprofits utilize many campaign tactics, like membership drives, pledging programs, mail appeals, major gift campaigns, canvassing, phone appeals, etc. They may also seek grants or contributions (including payroll giving or gift matching) from corporates, foundations, government, or other agencies: businesses, religious, civic, or community groups.

Your belief in your cause must overcome the discomfort of asking someone for money. Remember who you are truly raising funds for—the beneficiaries of your work and the communities you serve. Make the case larger than your nonprofit. Highlight how individuals and communities will be positively impacted—whether through new educational opportunities, economic development, community pride, or improved quality of life. Show how a donation is an investment in a brighter future.

ARE THERE CERTAIN RULES ON HOW MUCH FUNDRAISING A NONPROFIT CAN DO?

In fact, public charities must derive at least a third of their support from the public. In other words, your organization cannot rely too much on contributions that come from people closely involved with it, such as founders, board members, or employees. This is another reason why it is important to prioritize fundraising. It is also beneficial to diversify your revenue base. Receiving income from a wide range of donors and partners is a good thing for your organization's financial health.

HOW DOES A NONPROFIT GET REGISTERED TO FUNDRAISE?

There are certain requirements of nonprofits when it comes to raising funds from the general public. These requirements and regulations are meant to provide transparency for donors, providing protection from potential fraud or misrepresentation. They also allow nonprofits to minimize their tax obligations.

Not all states require registration before you begin to raise funds there. Some types of nonprofits are exempt from state registration, such as certain educational, religious, or membership organizations; revenue criteria may also be applicable. And if you have recently created a nonprofit organization and are still awaiting your 501(c)(3) status, this will not necessarily prohibit you from beginning fundraising activities; however, contributions will not be tax-deductible until your nonprofit is officially recognized as a charity. That said, it may be preferable to wait until your official registration status is confirmed. It is always wise to check the requirements as they pertain to your circumstances and conduct research and planning in advance before getting started.

To register your nonprofit, start by doing so in the state where you are based. You will need to submit a registration statement and supporting documentation to each state agency. You will typically be asked for basic information about your nonprofit and its finances, and potentially, officers or directors; most of this will then be available to the public. You can then proceed to register in any other states where you have a physical presence or where you might solicit donations.

WHAT DO WE NEED TO KNOW ABOUT RAISING FUNDS BEYOND STATE LINES?

When raising funds across state boundaries, you must adhere to the rules in each state. Register your organization in every state where you will be asking for donations. This applies to online fundraisers, not just in-person fundraising. Running a national or digital campaign will require you to register in every single state. Some states accept the Unified Registration Statement, but given the varying requirements, deadlines, and fees across states, this may or may not save you time.

WHAT CAN WE DO TO ENSURE THE SUCCESS OF OUR FUNDRAISING CAMPAIGN?

In times gone by, many nonprofits relied on methods like telethons, phone appeals, direct mail, and collecting donations at events. Now, there are many more ways to get people involved. You can and should strategically solicit donations in many ways, especially now that the internet has opened up the entire world.

Start planning ahead, promoting your campaign early, and spreading the word. The more people who hear about it, the more success you are likely to have. Make full use of your database, of your existing supporters and stakeholders, and even local press and businesses. Getting coverage in the form of a news story can go a long way, as can posters or flyers displayed in high-traffic areas. Optimize your website, landing pages, and donation forms to capture interest and donations. Don't be afraid of oversaturating your social media or experimenting with advertising. Remember that people generally need to be exposed to a message multiple times before they are inclined to act on it.

Adapt your approach, tone, and messaging as needed based on the channel and audience. What you say on a flyer will differ from how you communicate in a short online video, or how you speak to a representative at a business or foundation about gaining their financial support. While we may think of fundraising as asking a stranger for money, this is not the ideal way to approach it. Where possible, it is preferable to cultivate a relationship before making the request (and certainly to continue to nurture it afterward).

HOW DO WE ENSURE THAT OUR CAMPAIGNING IS COMPLETELY LEGAL?

Every country's laws will differ, but a variety of resources offer in-depth guidelines on navigating fundraising laws as a nonprofit. For instance, refer to the US Council of Nonprofits, Gov.UK, or Australia's Funding Centre.

Here are a few general pointers to keep in mind. For in-person fundraisers, you must procure the appropriate license for any event you are holding. A permit is usually needed to hold a fundraising event in a public place, and the minimum age for street collectors is usually 16. If taking place on private property, which includes shopping centers, you need permission beforehand from the owner or manager. This also applies to collection boxes. A license is required to serve alcohol and may be needed for a game of chance, such as a raffle or auction.

For online fundraisers, you will need to comply with privacy and anti-spam laws, such as the CAN-SPAM Act. Ensure people have truly opted in before you email them and make it clear how they can unsubscribe. The state of California (California Consumer Privacy Act) and the European Union (General Data Protection Regulations) outline additional regulations you may need to account for and keep in mind. Always err on the side of caution to ensure compliance.

WHAT INFORMATION MUST WE INCLUDE IN OUR FUNDRAISING MATERIALS?

It is important to ensure your fundraising materials include any and all legally required information, such as your registered charity status or number, full name, and registered office address. In many states, you must tell prospective donors how they can obtain a copy of your nonprofit's official financial filings. In addition to the disclosures you are required to display, think more broadly about the impression your fundraising collateral will make on a donor.

There you have it: a comprehensive guide to strategies for successful fundraising. Use this as a reference you can return to at any point to refresh your memory or to find new ideas.

CONCLUSION

Nonprofits play an essential role in today's world. They provide vital resources and programs for people and causes that may not be served otherwise because they are not commercially profitable. In other words, nonprofits operate for the public good, and their work ensures healthier, stronger, and more vibrant communities for the future.

No matter what field you operate in, the size of your organization, or the length of your tenure—fundraising must be a top priority for your nonprofit, year after year. It is imperative to maintain focus on acquiring and retaining donors, continuing the tactics that have brought success, and experimenting with new ones to fuel further growth. When fundraising is at the forefront of your strategy, you are investing in the long-term health and sustainability of your organization. Financial stability is what will ensure your team can continue doing this work and making an impact.

Fundraising is not a mysterious black box endeavor. It simply boils down to understanding and connecting with donors, inspiring them to give, and investing in the ongoing relationship so they continue to stay connected and contribute. I have outlined seven key strategies here: partnerships, bringing in donors, online fundraisers, campaigns, annual giving, event hosting, and donor retention and stewardship. You will have noticed that the key principles underlying all these are similar, as these are universal.

Every strategy begins with deliberate planning. Get clear on your goal. How much do you want to raise? What are you fundraising for? Why would someone want to give? Set specific, measurable, realistic objectives. Aim high, but don't overreach. Success breeds success, and with each win, you can expand your horizon further.

Lead by centering your audience, always keeping them at the forefront of any initiative. Understanding who they are and what they are interested in should inform everything about how you interact with them. This applies not just to your core campaign message, but also to the channels or platforms you use to communicate with them. Go where they are, rather than trying to get them to come to you. The more you do this, the higher the likelier reward.

Once you decide on what type of fundraiser to host, you will need to dive into the next level of detail. How much will this cost? What is the timeline? What resources are needed to execute? Make use of nonprofit technology to streamline workflow and automate tasks and try your hand at some of the popular fundraising platforms available today—like Fundly, Donately, Qgiv, and others listed earlier. Follow up with donors to express thanks. Always be upfront about where the funds are going. Whether someone gives $10 or $1,000, they desire and deserve to know how it will be used. So, whether their donation will fund a new animal shelter, books for underprivileged youth, or clean drinking water for families, get specific and give them a tangible image to connect to. Set the tone for your ongoing communication upfront, and then follow through with regular updates that help build trust, credibility, and the relationship.

Conduct a debrief after the fundraiser concludes to analyze the results. This allows for both celebration of successes and identifying opportunities to improve. Finally, I encourage you to treasure your team, both staff and volunteers. They are the engine of your fundraising efforts. And great leaders who have the heart and drive to raise substantial funds are a rare breed. Never take their effort for granted.

Now that you understand what fundraising is truly about and the tools it takes to successfully solicit donations for your nonprofit, you too have what it takes to execute the next Ice Bucket Challenge or March of Dimes. As you reach the end of this book, please consider writing a review online and sharing your honest opinion. If it has helped you in some way, then many more organizations out there could also benefit from hearing about it. Fundraising is a foundational pillar for any nonprofit; mastering this skill and incorporating the strategies outlined in this book will enable you to bring your mission to life at a larger scale. Keep this book as a guide —a blueprint as you continue on your fundraising journey—as the tools and strategies shared here are timeless principles you can continue to leverage regardless of the economic environment, year after year.

I hope you found the complete *Nonprofit Fundraising Mastery 2-in-1 Collection* beneficial and insightful. Your feedback is vital to me and the reader community. If this collection was helpful to you, I'd appreciate it if you could take a few moments to share your thoughts and leave a review on Amazon or Audible. Your contributions go a long way in helping me continually improve. Thank you for your time and support!

REFERENCES

ALS. (2021). ALS Ice Bucket Challenge Commitments. https://www.als.org/ice-bucket-challenge-spending.

America's Charities. Facts & Statistics on Workplace Giving, Matching Gifts, and Volunteer Programs.Bloomerang. (2022). Actually, Calling Donors To Thank Them Does Make Them More Likely To Give Again (And Give More). https://bloomerang.co/blog/actually-calling-donors-to-thank-them-does-make-them-more-likely-to-give-again-and-give-more/.

Bloomerang. (2022). A Guide to Donor Retention. https://bloomerang.co/blog/donor-retention/.

Candid. (2020). Key Facts on U.S. Nonprofits and Foundations. https://www.issuelab.org/resources/36381/36381.pdf

Double The Donation. (2022). Corporate Giving and Matching Gift Statistics. https://doublethedonation.com/matching-gift-statistics.

Donorbox. (2022). 13 Steps to The Perfect Year-End Giving Campaign in 2022.https://donorbox.org/nonprofit-blog/year-end-giving .

Ebarb, T. (2019). Nonprofits Fail – Here's Seven Reasons Why. National Association of Nonprofit Organizations & Executives (NANOE). https://nanoe.org/nonprofits-fail/.

Ewing Marion Kauffman Foundation. (2017). Nonprofit Effectiveness Initiative Research: Online Survey of Nonprofit Organizations – Report of Findings.https://www.kauffman.org/wp-content/uploads/2019/09/2017_Kauffman_Nonprofit_Effectiveness_Survey_Report_pdf.pdf

Finch, J. (2015). Fundraising Management Software User Report. Software Advice. https://www.softwareadvice.com/nonprofit/userview/fundraising-management-report-2015

Finch, J. (2015). Which Fundraising Event Is Best for Your Nonprofit? Software Advice.https://www.softwareadvice.com/nonprofit/industryview/fundraising-event-report-2015/

Georgia Tech. (2014). Face It: Instagram Pictures With Faces are More Popular. https://news.gatech.edu/news/2014/03/20/face-it-instagram-pictures-faces-are-more-popular

Network for Good. (2018). 7 Reasons Why Donors Give (and 1 Reason They Don't). https://www.networkforgood.com/resource/7-reasons-why-donors-give/.

Nonprofit Source. (2022). The Ultimate List Of Charitable Giving Statistics For 2022. https://nonprofitssource.com/online-giving-statistics/.

Orlando, A. (2021). 4 Nonprofit Fundraising Tips You'll Need in 2022. Donor Perfect. https://www.donorperfect.com/nonprofit-technology-blog/fundraising-software/strategize-by-season-4-nonprofit-fundraising-tips-youll-need-in-2022/

Ostrower, F. (2005). Stanford Social Innovation Review. The Reality Underneath the Buzz of Partnerships. https://ssir.org/articles/entry/the_reality_underneath_the_buzz_of_partnerships

Perrin, A. & Atske, S. (2021). About three-in-ten U.S. adults say they are 'almost constantly' online. Pew Research. https://www.pewresearch.org/fact-tank/2021/03/26/about-three-in-ten-u-s-adults-say-they-are-almost-constantly-online/

Philanthropy News Digest. (2018). Recurring Donors 440 Percent More Valuable Than 'One-Off' Donors. https://philanthropynewsdigest.org/news/recurring-donors-440-percent-more-valuable-than-one-off-donors

Statista. (2022). Most popular social networks worldwide as of January 2022, ranked by number of monthly active users. https://www.statista.com/statistics/272014/global-social-networks-ranked-by-number-of-users/

Steel, Emily. (2014). Ice Bucket Challenge Has Raised Millions for ALS Association. The New York Times. http://nytimes.com/2014/08/18/business/ice-bucket-challenge-has-raised-millions-for-als-association.html

Suttie. J., & Marsh, J. (2010). 5 Ways Giving is Good for You. Greater Good Magazine. https://greatergood.berkeley.edu/article/item/5_ways_giving_is_good_for_you

Wordstream. (2022). Google Ads Benchmarks For Your Industry. https://www.wordstream.com/blog/ws/2016/02/29/google-adwords-industry-benchmarks